FORWARD

The purpose of this book is to bring hope to the hopeless and to show the transforming power of Christ's love. I hope it encourages mothers to be persistent in prayer for their children, people to understand a mother's love, fathers to surrender first to Jesus and then to their children, and children to submit to their parents, in order that their love can be bigger, and they can all be together.

This book is not just to explain Jesus nailed to a cross. Instead, it endeavors to explain what Jesus nailed to a cross can mean to you today. For the lost children, the desperate mothers with hearts that have been pierced, the broken fathers unable to mend their lives, for the abused who suffer in silence, for the addicts trapped in a world dominated by fear, for the faithless to find faith, the hopeless to find hope, and for a church that I pray can open its doors and knock down its walls to embrace the one thing that never dies—love.

I would like to thank all who helped me move from a place of despair to hope in Christ.

Michael Fleming

Michael Fleming/Lee Cook

POWER IN THE NAME OF JESUS

A story of hope, redemption and answered prayers

Michael Fleming/Lee Cook

Author Name
Michael Fleming and Lee Cook

ISBN-13 978-1-6998324-3-1

INTRODUCTION

In the fall of 2014, Michael "Mick" Fleming began his first year of studies at Nazarene Theological College in Didsbury, Manchester, England and I began the first of a four-year term as a support volunteer at this small college with an incredible global impact. Students come from all over the world and from many denominations to be equipped to serve the church as they pursue their undergraduate and advanced degrees. A deep sense of community promotes a closeness among all involved. It was in this setting that I met Mick and watched his story unfold.

I relished watching Mick interact and care for people of all ages and all nationalities and go beneath the surface to find the greater need. I witnessed his love for all his family, his heart for his children, and his desire for them to know the blessings of living a godly life.

Mick's almost always instant obedience to the Holy Spirit's prompting in his life, his willingness to be completely transparent in order that others might understand the transforming power of God's amazing love, and the selfless ways Mick pours out his life and his resources to minister to others challenged my own daily walk with God.

He described himself as a man who had once been filled with pride, selfish ambition, unbelief, bitterness, violence, addictions, and crime. I witnessed, instead, a tender, gentle, forgiving, loving, giving, law-abiding, and self-disciplined man who reached out in ways that positively impacted all with whom he came in contact. He certainly inspired those of us who shared his journey at Nazarene Theological College!

The more I learned about the dramatic changes God had made in Mick's life, the more I became convinced that his was a story that needed to be told. Each time I heard about the amazing life-changing stories that developed through Mick's love and determination to serve God, the wonder of God's redemptive power greatly inspired and blessed me. And as I shared, with his permission, the way God was working through him, Mick's story deeply moved others, who, in turn, requested that his story be shared.

As Mick shared the events in this book, we became aware of the power of Mick's mother's prayers for him. For twenty years prior to her death she wrote heart-felt prayers seeking God's intervention in his life. Although she died without seeing the results of her prayers, the power of prayer became obvious in the ways God was at work in encounters which happened while Mick was a still a homeless addict and by follow-up encounters after Mick was clean and sober. May Mick's story bring you renewed hope in your time of deepest despair and greatest doubt.

My prayer is that all who read this book will hear Mick's heart, experience his love for God and others, and be inspired to develop their own personal relationship with a God who loves beyond measure and desires to share His love with all who will receive it and allow Him to bring healing to their lives and relationships. May you know fully God's love and plans for you. It is a life worth living—and it CAN be yours! There is STILL power in the name of Jesus! Jesus never changes; He was, He is, and He ever will be the Son of God who willingly gave His life so that we can be forgiven and experience a deeply personal relationship with Him.

Lee Cook

Note: This book was co-authored by a man from England and a woman from the United States, but it is the story of an English-man. Therefore, English spellings and expressions are used throughout, with footnotes for those not familiar with English expressions.

CONTENTS

PART ONE

Background and Early Years

Three loud explosions filled the air as I turned from the sparsely populated motorway[1] onto the slip road one morning about 3:00 a.m. I had a quick glimpse of a passenger with a baseball cap and a scarf around his face in the car that had pulled up beside me and which was now speeding away. I realized three shots had been fired into my car: one through the window and two through the door panel but all had missed me. Such was the state of my mind and the lack of spirituality that there was no fear. I began to laugh and as I looked in the rear-view mirror, I saw my eyes were filled with disdain. I couldn't stop laughing as I followed the car, saying over and over, "It's time to die!" I can't really describe the emotions I felt then in relation to what I know about myself now. I did take vengeance—not to the point of killing—but I did take vengeance. At the time I felt totally justified and even empowered. I felt empowered by acts of evil because I didn't see them as evil; they were just normal. I now realize that the laughter was demonic. Not only was I not with God, I was with something else. I enjoyed the adventure of someone trying to kill me because I knew I could take vengeance.

Fast-forward thirty years. I had been to an event with a friend, a new Christian who was struggling with anger and resentment from his past. As we were driving home, I started to turn off the motorway at the wrong exit and, when I realized it, swerved back onto the motorway, narrowly missing being hit by

---

[1] A wide road for fast-moving traffic, with a limited number of places at which drivers can enter and leave it

the traffic behind me. I was entirely to blame. The man behind me had to pull off because I had inadvertently cut him off. The man was obviously angry, and I raised my hand to apologise. However, my passenger, who was already upset by something that had happened previously, began to swear and make unpleasant gestures at the man. The man went around the rotary[2] and came back onto the motorway behind me. He pulled alongside my driver's side and presented a handgun turned sideways, pointed at me. I pulled back and the man slowed down and then pulled the gun up twice more. I knew the man was trying to intimidate me, so I just gently smiled and shrugged my shoulders and tilted my head toward my passenger. From that point on the man followed us rather than being alongside. My friend didn't see the handgun or the gesture, he only saw the man pulling alongside. I made the decision not to tell my friend. It was dark and he had not seen what was going on. However, he was still seething with anger and ready to jump out of the car and attack the other man.

At this point I began praying and realized that I didn't feel any fear, but I also didn't feel any anger. Clearly, as I was praying, I heard God speaking to me, saying, "You've been both these men. Who's in the driver's seat now?" I replied, "You are Lord."

We pulled up to a traffic light where the man could have jumped out. My passenger was trying to remove his seatbelt, but I softly told him to keep it on. I felt God was in total control. After following us for another few miles the man turned off and was gone. I dropped off my friend and never told him what had

---

[2] Intersection in which the traffic moves in one direction round a central island

happened with the gun. When he was getting out of the car, I reminded him that it was important to learn to not respond with swearing and anger. He confessed it was something he struggled with and couldn't seem to stop.

As I was driving home, thanking God I caught my eyes in the rear-view mirror again. This time I felt nothing but love. I prayed for the man that had been following us and prayed for my friend because I knew I had been both. I prayed that the Lord would speak to them as He had spoken to me.

When I got home, I received a text message from my friend apologising for his behavior. I responded that we all need to learn as we walk our journey.

When the car had pulled up alongside, I remembered when I had previously been shot at and the emotions I experienced at that time, compared to the emotions I felt this night. I felt the effects of evil on both sides but recognized the evil now had no power over me. I had no need to react but recognized how the impact of evil could spread. One bad action could have spread to a bad reaction, which would have impacted everyone and everything around it. On the other hand, the power of Christ being in the middle of two bad reactions was able to disperse the power of evil. It had taken many years for me to learn this lesson…

I grew up in an Irish Catholic family. My father, Hugh Fleming, was the child of staunch Catholic immigrant parents.

He was taught to attend and support the church. His was a religion of duty but he had no personal relationship with Jesus.

Dad was a hard-working man. He was very strict, stern, and went to church every Sunday. I was the only boy in the family and had four sisters. I always felt that Dad expected more of me. He wanted me to be tougher and stronger--but when I was, he didn't really like it. Although a good man, in those early years there was a sternness and coldness about Dad that separated him from his children. He was not violent or abusive; he just never displayed warmth to us. Our mother, on the other hand, was a great nurturer.

At the age of eleven, I was an innocent child, very much a mummy's boy. One morning on the way to school I was attacked and brutally raped. At that point, my whole world changed. I went on to school, pretending the attack and rape had not happened, in shock-- bleeding inside--but told nobody. After school I ran home and upstairs to my room without telling my parents. I was very scared, and as I lay crying during the night, biting the covers so no one would hear my crying, I decided I would tell my parents what had happened in the

---

[3] Years later, after I was clean and sober and helping others with addictions, I met the man who had attacked me as a child. For two years I worked to help him on the road to sobriety. In that time, I actually began to like him as a person. With God's help I was eventually able to forgive him. He died within a few years of our meeting. I never revealed to him that he had attacked me as a child. I know that I was able to forgive him only through the power of Jesus. I am grateful that God brought him back into my life and enabled me to forgive him.

morning. Little did I know that those were the last tears I would shed for thirty-four years! [3]

As I came downstairs the following morning, prepared to tell my parents what had happened, my dad was coming into the house and said, "Your sister's dead!" The screams from my mother and the sight of my dad crying made me freeze. I didn't know what to do. I learned that my sister had an asthma attack. Our dad had caught her in his arms and rushed her to the steps of the hospital. She was twenty years of age when she died in our father's arms.

I just couldn't add to my family's grief by telling them what had happened to me the previous morning. That day was the start of many years of addiction for me. I knew that my mother took pain tablets for her back and I began to sneak her medications to help me cope with my pain. This decision triggered a long path in which I took a variety of drugs for the next thirty-four years; and became progressively worse in my addictions.

In keeping with Irish Catholic tradition, the coffin for my sister was placed in our front room. Men would come around to visit and drink and on one night about twenty men began reciting the rosary together. I was upstairs and frightened by the chanting. It didn't sound like a God thing to me; I was petrified! Interestingly, as my dad later recalled the event, he said it was his first experience of feeling the love of Christ. In the midst of the men praying the rosary, my dad prayed, "Lord, take this cup from me, but Your will be done." At that moment Dad remembered feeling an overwhelming feeling of peace, love, and joy. He also felt very guilty for feeling these emotions when his family was suffering. My dad knew there was more to faith than he had experienced, more than the way he had been brought up in the church, but he had no idea how to find it. Eventually my dad returned to living as he had been prior to my sister's death. He wouldn't speak about her death. Once when I brought up the subject, Dad closed me down, he wouldn't speak about it.

My parents' marriage somehow became stronger after the loss of their daughter and their faith grew as well. My mother found a personal relationship with Jesus and became a Spirit-filled, charismatic Catholic. My life, on the other hand, turned to pursuing money, drugs, and power--living a criminal lifestyle--and I was devoid of all emotion.

I married when I was 18 and she was 17. She was expecting at the time of our marriage. During the early years we were very poor. However, even though we lacked money to buy nappies[4], I could still find enough money to buy alcohol. I remember feeling so useless and guilty for drinking, knowing how much it upset my lovely wife who worked hard to look after our children, Matthew and Daniel.

At this point in my life, I had no faith. I made a conscious decision to get more money. Instead of stopping spending money on the things that were wrong in my life, I decided to do

---

[4] Diapers

whatever it took to make enough money to take care of my children and wife and still be able to do the things I wanted to do. I made a conscious decision to become a criminal; it was not something into which I drifted. Sadly, I consciously chose this route.

I found something that I was good at--or so I thought at the time. I became involved in all kinds of shady deals. Very quickly I developed an amazing lifestyle—if, in fact, an amazing lifestyle is defined by bigger cars and houses, better clothes, and fancier jewelry.

The downside to this kind of life was the affect that it had on my family which I honestly couldn't see at the time. Our home was raided by the police many times, at all times of the day and night. These raids had a profound effect on my wife and our growing children. I definitely wish I could go back and change these experiences. I know I can't and have had to accept the fact that I did these things and I was the one who brought these terrible consequences on my family.

I loved my children so much! I almost idolized them. I think I tried to turn them into people like me. I tried to teach my sons not to accept authority and deliberately worked to instill in them hatred toward the police. My wife could clearly see what I was doing and tried to stop me. I wouldn't listen, convinced that I knew best.

My wife became pregnant for the third time and we were absolutely delighted! We were hoping for a little girl. We had built everything up so quickly. I felt I was responsible for creating this family, that I was going to look after and nurture them, and that nobody was going to tell me what was right and wrong. My wife lost the baby. I remember she was lying in the bed after the doctor had been in. I was devastated--but not for her--for myself. As I recall the experience today, I feel so ashamed that I couldn't even put my arms around her to help her through that most difficult time. I didn't have the ability then to love outside of myself, to empathise with others.

As the months passed following the loss of the baby, our family slowly returned to the routine where I did whatever I pleased, made as much money as possible and expected all the family to be grateful. The boys were playing football and boxing, and I began to spend all my spare time with the boys in pursuit of their sports. I completely neglected my wife— especially her emotional needs as a mother and a wife.

She became pregnant again. We were over the moon, but this time a little bit cautious. Everything went well, and we had a beautiful daughter, Elle-Ann! It seemed to me that our family was complete. I felt I had the boys and my wife had a girl. In my mind I would do the boy stuff and she would do the girlie stuff.

At this point, money wasn't too much of a problem, but we were arguing more and more. I made a conscious decision not to drink or take drugs anymore. I stuck to that for quite some time. I used my own will power and prayed to the god of money to help me through. The problem was that I became more obsessed with other things! I wanted to have our children dress better than others, I was obsessed about what my wife and I should be doing; I became obsessive in my behavior patterns. That obsession kept me sober but everyone around me could see that it was as destructive as the drugs and alcohol had been.

By the time Elle was about three, my wife was suffering from severe postnatal depression which eventually required hospitalization.

We later divorced and the children lived with me for a time. My bitterness over the breakup and her illness made me single-minded and resentful toward her. I made it very difficult for her to have a good relationship with the children. Things have worked out over the years despite my actions. I am truly sorry for the part I played in the divorce and for what happened afterwards.

As life progressed my addiction was on and off, gradually becoming permanently on and eventually I ended up in a psychiatric ward. My predicament was self-inflicted by drugs.

Reconciliation is difficult and slow because of all the emotional issues for everybody involved. I know my children have been deeply affected by my behavior and by my response to life. I pray that one day they can completely forgive me and understand. I hope that one day things can heal for them; that they can forgive me; that their lives can be blessed, and they can learn by my huge mistakes. These three wonderful children have become independent, caring, and reliable adults— everything I was *not* in those days.

I later remarried and had a third son, Jack, with my second wife. Although that marriage also ended in divorce, I am so grateful that I have had an opportunity to bond with Jack during his formative years and model the difference Christ can make in a life yielded to Him.

I see my broken family slowly being restored through the love that I inherited through my faith in Jesus and especially through the love that my father, in his later years, was able to extend to his children and grandchildren. Blame is over, guilt doesn't hold me down. I simply want to learn to love them all in the way they deserve, and I am trying to do that with the help of my Lord and Saviour Jesus Christ, because I know there is no other way.

The biggest change to my family came when my mom passed away. It was a change for the entire family but especially for my dad. However, I blamed my dad. I truly don't know why, but the focus for the hatred I felt became directed toward my father. No matter what my father might have done or said, he could not have done anything to make it better—it was me and not my dad.

Soon after my mother died my father was hospitalized with cancer with a fifty-fifty chance of living. When I went to see my father, I cursed him to his face and told him I hoped he would die. They were not just words; I meant it. There was no relationship left between my dad and me because I wouldn't allow it. Dad recovered. He sold his home and moved into a small flat. I stole most of the money from the sale of the house and justified it by the hatred I felt for my father. I felt no guilt or shame at the time. I remember thinking it was a good thing.

Time had passed and even though I had done these horrible things to my father, I realized I didn't have anything that had belonged to my mother. I didn't have any money left and my addiction was spiraling to new lows. I went to see my dad and asked him for something that had belonged to my mom. I was hoping for jewelry or something I could sell to buy drugs. My dad said there is nothing; your sisters have it all, there is nothing left. He then said, "You can take this" and passed me my mother's Bible. I became angry. Why would I want a Bible? I didn't even believe in God! But I took it for only one reason--so my dad wouldn't have it! It was a few more years before I opened that Bible but when I did, I was astonished at what I found in the back of the book! The personal hand-written prayers that my mother had been praying for me for over twenty years prior to her death were all there in front of me. There were photographs, newspaper clippings, highly personal things, all relating to me. Dad had never looked in the Bible; he didn't know they were there.

In thinking back over the dark times, I have come to realize that Mum's prayers *were* being answered—even though it wasn't obvious at the time. Strangely, in times when I was at rock bottom, God somehow still used me to profoundly impact the lives of strangers in a positive way. After I was clean and sober, God graciously brought some of those people back into my life to share the impact of these initial encounters.

One of those encounters occurred when I was still drinking and using; I didn't have any faith. I was sitting behind a supermarket, shaking, and drinking cider from a bottle. I was just getting to the place where the shakes were stopping. It was near Christmas and very cold.

I was approached by a young man and lady and the man had a pen and a pad. They seemed like nice, respectable people. The man said, "Can we ask you some questions?" I asked him why and he said he needed answers for a course he was doing for his degree. I agreed to answer if he would give me a cigarette. The man gave the lady some money and sent her to the shop to get some cigarettes and a lighter.

While she was gone, he told me he had only two questions: 1) What it felt like to live the life I was living, and 2) What I thought the future held for me. He said these were the only two questions he wanted to ask, and would it be all right if he took notes while I talked? To be honest, all I wanted was the cigarettes: I didn't really care what the man wanted. We waited until the lady came back, I lit a cigarette and began to feel nice and relaxed. The man repeated the two questions. I asked if I could have the pad and pen and I wrote on the pad. I wrote very quickly. I didn't have any control over what I was writing, I had no clue what I was writing! I filled the page up in what seemed like seconds. I didn't even read it but just handed the pad back to the man. The man and lady hovered over it, reading it for themselves. The lady began to cry, and as the man held her in his arms, the two of them cried together. They thanked me, shook my hand and left.

I forgot the incident until about four years later when I was clean and sober, sitting in a drug and alcohol centre, having a coffee. A man I didn't recognize came and introduced himself. He sat down and told me we had met before. He turned out to be the man with the pad on which I had written. The man had become a qualified drug and alcohol worker. He said the words that I wrote that day had changed his life and made him feel that the job he was doing now was not just a job, but a vocation. He thanked me. I smiled and asked him, "What were the words? I don't know." The man said, "Give me your email and I will send them to you."

When I read what I had written I could see the despair and the hopelessness in the words but knew that they were beyond my own capability to compose. I couldn't believe they came from my hand. I've kept those words on my phone as a reminder of my previous despair. Following are the words I wrote that day in response to the two questions while I sat, addicted, on the street behind the supermarket:

"The cold wind wraps around his body like a spiteful lover. The dark echo of his breath slowly disappearing into a distant silence. The familiar smell of an old friend who would never desert him lay heavy on his breath. A home on the street, but no door and never a key. Once a father, never a son. Flashes of a man that never was. A victim from the age of 11, a child that forgot how to cry. Nightmares that unpacked but would never leave. To sleep, to smile, to feel the touch of humanity were all things for others. Finding a god in a needle and love in a pipe. How much longer? He asks for nothing and receives it in abundance.

Flashing lights, a strange unfamiliar warmth, distant voices. A brilliant blinding blackness. No one to cry, no one to leave flowers, a nameless faith, neither forgotten nor

*remembered. Then the wind blew again, and they all turned
away. Merry Christmas."*

I could never have written these words at that point in my life.
I couldn't even do it now, not in seconds. It makes me very
grateful to know that God was with me and using me to impact
others even when I didn't personally know God. Recalling this
story may have been the first time I consciously realized that my
mother's prayers were being answered, even though she
couldn't see the results

I was well into addiction, using class A drugs[5] every day,
along with alcohol. My lifestyle up to this point had been a
criminal lifestyle of violence, enjoying the power that came from
doing my own thing, not realizing the damage being done.

In my late twenties I had made a pact saying, "If I can have a
lot of money and power you can do what you want with me." I
wasn't consciously making a pact with the devil as I had no
regard for my soul. The money and power came. I would write
spells—what I wanted to happen to a person—and it would
happen. I didn't even realize I was practicing witchcraft.

Although I was getting power from the dark, I began to feel
empty. The money and power were now producing only a huge
emptiness. So, I used more and more drugs, more and more
alcohol, to fill that empty feeling. As a result, I became more
dangerous as I was becoming increasingly psychotic from the
drugs I was taking. I became more and more violent, very

---

[5] Class A drugs in the UK include: Crack cocaine, Crystal meth; Cocaine,
Ecstasy; Heroin; LSD; Magic mushrooms

intimidating, people couldn't be around me for too long, I was too dangerous.

As my addiction reached its worst, I remember turning up at Dad's door, absolutely drenched. I was living on the streets and there was no way of getting dry. I was drenched, cold, and miserable. Dad shut the door in my face. I knew I had nowhere else to go, nowhere else to turn. I have since learned that my Dad and sisters had come together and determined they could do nothing more for me. They had done everything they could to help me and they thought I was dying because of the way I looked and how I was living my life. They were just waiting for the phone call to tell them I had died.

Through the heavy drug use I lost my riches; I could not hold myself or a house together. I was just living in the moment as I was going insane from the drugs. To get money I began collecting drug debts—the dealers would pay me to collect large debts. I was offered a large amount of money to kill someone with a large debt. There was a partial payment first and the rest would come after. I had quite a lot of money in my pocket, a stolen car, a gun, and went to take the man's life.

I waited for the man outside of a gym. I was so erratic that I hadn't checked for cameras or anything—it was not a clever plan. I had no fear, there was a coldness about me for what I was doing, I was already blaming the man for his own death. There were no emotions. All feelings had disappeared. The gun, inside a carrier bag[6], was not visible. I jumped out of the car as the man walked out of the gym. As the man walked

---

[6] A plastic or paper bag with handles

toward me, all I could see was his hands holding his little daughters' hands on either side. I could only see those hands; I couldn't see anything else. At that point I started feeling something I couldn't remember feeling before. I didn't understand what was happening and I was confused. I couldn't kill the man; I just couldn't do it.

I got back in the car and drove off to an industrial estate where it was very quiet. I still couldn't understand why I couldn't do it; I was in shock about what was happening, I had never felt anything like I was feeling. I started to shake and as I was shaking the feeling got really strong inside me. I knew it was a good feeling, but I didn't want it. I tried to push it away, but it just got stronger and stronger. Instinctively I grabbed the gun, put it under my chin, and pulled the trigger—it did not go off. It just did not go off.

I earnestly prayed for the first time I could remember since I was a little boy. I prayed for God to help me for I didn't realize what I had become. For just a few seconds while praying I vividly remember Johnny Cash singing "Man in Black" on the car radio. I felt I was the man in black but didn't feel it was a tribute to God—I felt dark. I remember thinking that somehow there must be a way to take this "black suit" off so that is what I prayed for. I was starting to feel withdrawals from the drugs and alcohol I had used earlier. I went to get rid of the car and the gun. But before I disposed of the gun in the field, I shot it three times and it fired all three times. I prayed a second prayer, to thank God, for I knew God had kept me alive against my own will and in that moment, I was very grateful.

I got back in my own car and was driving in my hometown when I was stopped by the police. They arrested me on a previous warrant for a minor offence. After being arrested I was taken straight to court. I was very destructive and abusive in the courtroom and asked the judge to send me to jail. The judge said he was not accustomed to giving people what they want and gave me a fine instead, warning me about my behavior in the courtroom.

I felt so low that I didn't even want to walk out of the door into the sunshine, I just wanted everything to go away--everything. As I walked out, I lit up a cigarette in the building. I knew it was illegal, but didn't care, I was used to doing just what I wanted. A security guard snatched it from me. I hit him and knocked him unconscious and calmly lit up another cigarette and walked away. Before I got to the door I was surrounded by policemen and forcibly arrested. I got what I wanted-- I was locked in a cell! When they came to interview me about the offense, they were exceptionally nice, talking softly and quietly, and it became apparent that something more was going on. They told me they wanted me to speak to a doctor. I told them I would if they gave me cigarettes. They did, taking me out to the yard to smoke.

Instead of going to jail I was sent forcibly to a psychiatric unit. The doctors and police believed I was a danger to society since I was suffering from drug induced psychosis. They felt I was so unstable that I was likely to harm someone else or myself.

I thank God for the experience of the psychiatric unit. I had nothing when I walked through the doors but the people who were mentally ill, the patients, gave me clean clothes, training shoes, cigarettes, everything I needed. These people with a wide variety of mental health diagnoses loved me. I felt accepted and I felt equal for the first time in my life, without even trying.

A Catholic nun used to visit the psychiatric ward. I would go to her and she would pray for me. I always felt a peace that I had not felt before. I wanted that peace; I really, really wanted that feeling of peace. I was monitored twenty-four hours a day and not allowed to go out. I spent a lot of time writing, drawing, just scribbling, not aware of what I was writing. I wrote some numbers down; they were just random numbers because I was ill. One of the other patients, who too was very ill, saw the numbers and said those numbers are from the Bible. I just laughed. The other man went and got a Bible and opened it to Matthew chapters five through seven which were the numbers and we read it together. It was the Sermon on the Mount and I believe that was the beginning of the change in my life.

I found that portion of scripture on You-Tube and listened to it every night. I thought if I can just do what He says, I will be all right. But there was the bit about tearing out your own eye and cutting off your own hand and I thought, "I am not doing that!"

The next time the nun came to see me, I asked her what it meant, and she told me it was symbolic and explained in a way I could understood what the beatitudes were and what they meant. I asked her if God could love someone, even someone like me? She answered, "Especially somebody like you!" I felt special in that moment. Because I had done so many bad things, I didn't actually feel forgiven then, but I did feel loved. I was certain I was going to get better and have a life. I was no longer desperate.

I was in the mental hospital for about four months during which time I had no contact with family or friends. I was afraid to leave but I didn't want to be there. I was becoming institutionalized even in the short time I was there. Eventually, I was allowed to go out on my own to smoke, but I was afraid to even step over the edge of the walk. I felt secure in the institution since I knew how bad the world really was.

A man who was a part-time pastor and also a volunteer with drug and alcohol services came to help me fill out forms so I could receive services to help with my addictions. I was the first person he had visited as a volunteer. Years later he told me that he cried after he left because of how ill I was. I thought I was okay at the time. This man continued to pray for me every day, but I didn't know that until years later when we met in a McDonalds restaurant. [7]

One day a new patient came into the psychiatric unit, he was the tallest man I had ever seen, over seven feet tall. This new patient paced around the unit, and I could tell he was building himself up to be violent so kept an eye on him. He disappeared from my vision for a second and then I felt a choking sensation. The man had gone behind me and was using a belt to strangle me. I instantly felt myself becoming the "old me"; instantly the old anger and violent nature returned. Hospital employees tried to pull the explosive patient off me, but the man refused to loosen the belt. I received a super strength and managed to remove the tormentor. I initially responded very violently but,

---

[7] The story of that meeting appears later in this book.

suddenly, I knew that I had to stop. I had never experienced anything like this before, but something had stopped me.

The next day the doctors included me in a meeting. In my mind, I thought I would never be released, that I would be stuck in there. But the doctors informed me that I was as well as I could be, and if I stayed, I could revert to a prior condition, so it was time for me to be released.

Although I was pleased, I was also scared since I was clean and sober for the first time in so many years. I was leaving the hospital as an alcohol and drug free man—a condition I had not experienced for a long time. My biggest fear involved people seeing me with nothing; I feared they would see through this big shot that I had created in my own mind. My greatest fear was the result of my own pride.

I ended up in a homeless hostel, where staff members were very nice to me. While there, the thought came to me that perhaps there had always been nice people in the world, but I had never seen them before. I decided this was probably true!

I had no clue where I was going or what I was going to do. I prayed every day and every night for Jesus to come and show me what to do. One day as I was praying, an angel appeared at the bottom of my bed and the angel told me exactly where to go and what to do. The experience was very real to me. I was sober and was clean. Some people later told me that it could have been part of my former illness, but everything the angel told me happened as I was told. The angel returned for three consecutive days but has never appeared again. I remember feeling that I was not alone and that I was being looked after. Inside I felt cared for and certain that my life had purpose.

This interaction with the angel started me on a path to recovery which brought me to where I am today. My mother's prayers were being answered.

Though clean and sober and having had the experience with the angel who guided me directly and precisely to different situations and different people, my urge to use drugs and drink still was almost overwhelming. I was on the breaking point of going back to using alcohol and drugs when my angel visitor directed me exactly to a specific place I needed to go and where I needed to stand. It was about four minutes away from the homeless hostel. I had to be there at 7:00. While there waiting, I thought to myself, "I must be crazy doing this!"

I arrived about 6:55 and leaned against the wall where I was supposed to be. I lit a cigarette. The place where I was standing was close to the Manchester Town Hall which has a huge clock. As it chimed 7:00 a man walked toward me whom I recognized as a care worker in the homeless hostel. "Hi Mick, I bet you didn't expect to see me here." I replied, "No, what do you mean?" The man answered, "It's anonymous." I was completely baffled and didn't understand what the man meant. The care worker said, "Come in, I'll get you a coffee."

It turned out that the building to which I had been directed was where Alcoholics Anonymous (AA) meetings took place regularly. The care worker told me that he had once been an alcoholic and drug addict but had been clean for fifteen years.

He invited me to come and sit in the meeting and just listen and told me I didn't have to speak. I went in and listened. I don't remember much from that meeting other than one person saying, "We will love you until you can love yourself."

I began regularly attending meetings in various places. I would buy weekly bus passes and travel to the meetings. I soon learned that the basis for recovery for drug addicts and alcoholics was grounded in a belief in a higher power—or God. I felt compelled to ask myself, "Do I believe in God? Am I willing to believe in God?" I knew I believed in God; I was sure of it. I felt that the things I had experienced were possible only through God, so I knew there was a God. My prayers were to God, but not necessarily Jesus.

In the meetings I attended, conflicting opinions about spirituality and God arose as well as discussions regarding how to stay sober—everyone had a different opinion. I had not done the twelve steps yet. I wanted to do them because I was afraid I would return to using. I knew I couldn't stay clean and sober by myself and saw this as an opportunity.

To complete the twelve steps, I would need to find a sponsor-- someone who would mentor and take me through this process. A rigorous process; this experience lays its participants completely bare. As I attended the meetings, I noticed that everyone I saw was clean and sober, but some were happy and full of love, while others were not--they were just sober. I prayed and asked God what the difference was and immediately received the answer, "Jesus." The more I attended the meetings the more I began noticing those sounding as though they were Christians; there was a distinct difference between them and others. The Christian element of recovery seemed free whilst those people who accepted God without Christ were indeed sober and clean, they just weren't free. They were still trapped within themselves.

I then decided there was something about this Jesus that was very strong because I had physically seen it. I began to pray. At first, I prayed the same way I had always prayed but then I began tagging on to the end of my prayers, "Thank you God and Jesus."

During a conversation outside the meeting someone told me that Jesus was God. I went away and thought about that in light of my upbringing. I didn't feel confident in my understanding about this. How can Jesus be God if he was a man? Jesus couldn't be God. A few weeks later I found myself in the company of a man who was a pastor. The pastor said to me, "The Lord has told me to tell you about the trinity." I responded, "The Lord told me to tell you you're a nutter and to shut your gob[8]!" The pastor laughed and said, "If you accept what I am telling you, God is going to bless you for the rest of your life. But you don't have to listen to me if you don't want to." I thought being blessed for the rest of my life was worth a shot, so I decided to listen to him. It was a selfish reason for me to listen, but I listened.

The pastor told me about the Father, the Son, and the Holy Spirit. He said, "You are not meant to understand it; it's all right that you don't understand it. There's a power in you Mick that is ready to explode. Can I pray for you?" We were sitting in a

---

[8] Mouth

coffee place with a lot of people around us and I said, "No, I'm okay, thank you." The pastor said, "You know the funny thing Mick?" "What?" I asked. He said, "You can't stop me from praying for you." I responded, "No, I suppose not but I can get up and walk away." The pastor asked, "Are you walking away from me Mick, or are you walking away from God?" I felt like I had been punched in the stomach and my head literally just fell forward; the pastor had spoken the truth. The pastor went on, "I'm going to pray that someone will come along and say the right words at the right time. And I know my prayer is already answered." I could see how certain he was in his face as he smiled; there was no doubt, and we parted as friends.

The conversation stayed on my mind—not so much what the pastor had said as the fact that the pastor had no doubt. The pastor was already certain that what he had asked for was already answered. That just kept playing in my mind, and I wondered what it meant. I couldn't work it out of my mind. It just stayed and wouldn't go away. How could he be so certain? How is that even possible?

Within two days I had started to look for a sponsor required to complete the twelve steps since I knew it was what I needed to do. I was sitting in a meeting and heard a man sharing. I heard the words in my mind, "That's him." Then the man revealed he was gay. I said, "That's not him." Then the man revealed that he wasn't a Christian but believed in God. I said, "That's definitely not him." Again, the voice in my mind said, "No, Mick—that really is him." I didn't want to ask this gay, non-Christian to sponsor me. I was still slightly homophobic, but I had been praying and asking Jesus to help my understanding. I wore a big fancy cross around my neck as if saying, "Look at me! I'm a Christian!" I still, however, didn't understand and the message of the voice would not go away. I didn't know what to do so I did nothing. I didn't ask the man.

Every day for one full week that voice remained in my mind. It wouldn't go away. It was like being tortured, "Ask him! Ask him! Ask him!" It just wouldn't go away! So, I prayed, "Jesus, if this is the one I should ask to help me, then show me, and I'll do it." The minute I prayed I understood what the pastor said to me, I had prayed and didn't have any doubts at all. I felt I was having the same feeling as the pastor had. I was absolutely certain and knew that the man I was resisting would be my sponsor, and that he would take me through the twelve steps. I knew the prayer was already answered. I asked God what that meant, and the answer was, "Faith."

I thought I was beginning to understand what having faith in Jesus meant. I was about to do something that I didn't want to do but was doing it because I believed it was what God was directing me to do. I was trusting in God that it would all work out.

Within a week I saw the man at another meeting, which was unusual because I had never seen him except for that one time before. I asked him if he would sponsor me and he immediately said yes. The doubt returned to my mind as soon as I asked the man because he responded, "Oh, yeah, but I've never taken anyone through before." I thought, "I've just got a gay, non-Christian, who has never taken anyone through the steps before to sponsor me; I must be mad!"

We began the steps. Once a week the man would come to my house, and we would sit and have coffee and go through the process together. This is a scriptural process and it demands rigorous honesty. There is nowhere to hide. It goes deeper than any emotional counseling can possibly go. There were times in the process when I became physically sick as I faced myself in all my sin.

We came to step three which is handing your life and your will over to the care of God as you understand Him. At this point I asked my sponsor if it was all right if I handed my life and my will over to Jesus. The sponsor replied, "Yes, of course." At the end of this step you are handing everything you are, and all your being over to God. It is a total surrender of yourself. There's a prayer that you say that is drawn from Biblical scripture, that refers to God as Creator, but you can add to or subtract from that prayer; the prayer is a guide. I tailored the prayer and handed my life and will over to Jesus Christ, my Lord and Saviour. As I said the prayer, I started to feel warmth traveling through my body. As I started to breathe, I felt clear, and I felt my breathing was different.

Five minutes of silence follows the end of the prayer. In that silence I felt like I was literally dragged into another dimension. I felt my world was physically changing as I sat there. My mind was no longer running quickly from thought to thought to thought as it had done for so long, it was completely still. I felt like I was wrapped in a warm kind of blanket, protected and loved. I felt a peace in the room and as I was thanking God in my mind, I heard a quiet sobbing sound and realized that my sponsor was crying. As I opened my eyes the man said, "God is surely with us today." This was the experience that led me to accept God in Jesus Christ in a more permanent way. From that point on there really hasn't been room for any other kind of God for me.

As I went through the rest of the steps in the following weeks, I developed a new thirst for knowledge—the knowledge of God. By the time I had finished the twelve steps I could honestly say that my only wish, my burning ambition, and everything about me, was just wanting more of God. That part has remained constant in my life. I saw God and I continued seeking and wanting to carry out God's will. I was led to Christ by a gay, non-Christian man who showed me the love of Jesus on a level that I had never experienced. My sponsor laid himself down, put himself to one side, and allowed me to find Jesus. He didn't use his personal opinion; he didn't try to manipulate me to think what he wanted me to think; instead, he allowed God to do all of the work. This gay non-Christian man taught me how to evangelize. I now believe God uses everybody, so I try not to dismiss anyone because I may be dismissing God.

After completing the twelve steps, my life improved greatly, I now had a mechanism of rules in my life that I could follow that would to some extent, keep me connected to God. There was a blockage, however, in my relationship with Jesus since I was trying to pray my way to heaven; I was trying to do a lot of things to stay connected to God. I believed in God, and I believed in Jesus; but it was like someone I had been told about but that I had never really met.

I spent the next few years hoping to meet Him. I was a Christian, and I was trying so hard. I was staying sober and clean from drugs, but everything was tough. Everything was a battle. When I completed step three, I had surrendered my addiction. Several years later I surrendered myself.

My step three took about eight years to complete. The difference is that I no longer work the steps; instead, God works them for me. This is the fundamental difference in the Christian life. We must ask ourselves, "Is God, through the Holy Spirit, working in my life, or am I still trying to do it myself in the name of God?" When someone totally surrenders, he/she doesn't have to try anymore but just needs to be obedient.

I thought to myself, "My sponsor's not a Christian so I'll change him" but the truth is, my sponsor changed me. I ask myself, "How arrogant is it when we decide how God works and who He works through?" We must lose the arrogance and allow the Spirit to flow. We must be open-minded in the Spirit of Christ to understand how people believe and how people practice their faith.

Even though my sponsor had knowledge he wanted to give, he taught me from a place of equality. As I opened my life and laid everything out in the open, the sponsor did the same thing and that placed us on an equal plane. It is this humility of equality that has made a difference when I minister to others and it is something I learned from my sponsor. When I minister to someone I not only pray for that person, but I ask him/her to pray for me. I acknowledge my own need rather than appearing self-sufficient. This has allowed my ministry to be fruitful.

God used a non-Christian to teach me this approach and I have found this level of humility in service very rare. People who have suffered can come down to the level of other persons and meet them where they are. Christ's suffering on the cross allowed Him to come to our level of suffering and meet our needs. My sponsor understood my suffering and came down to meet me there, which in turn, transformed me. Christ understands our suffering because He came down to meet us where we are—and He longs to transform us.

God showed himself to me amidst my deepest misery, which followed soon after the incident where Dad closed the door in my face while I was still addicted and living on the street.

As I began to get better and was praying and understanding the love of God more, I knew that I had to repent of everything I had done and that I had to humble myself if I ever hoped to receive forgiveness; I was such a proud man. I began contacting the long list of people I had hurt. My dad was high on the list.

Finally, the day came when I went to see my dad. I was clean and sober, but also afraid. I laid myself bare and asked Dad to forgive me. I admitted everything I had done. For the first time in my life Dad told me that he loved me. A new relationship was born.

On Christmas day that year I had been clean and sober for about six months. For the first time in many years I was having a family meal with my dad and sisters. I was lying on the floor in front of the fire. Everyone was talking and laughing around me, but I felt completely separate from them, different.   I was experiencing emotional pain; it was being felt as physical pain in my stomach, but I knew really it was emotional pain. I was holding my stomach.

One of my sisters tried to encourage me, "You're doing really well. You haven't taken any drugs or been drinking. You're doing really well, and we are really proud of you."

I stood up, looked out the window and watched the rain coming down and the wind blowing the trees. I was sober for the first time in thirty-five years. But all I wanted to do was drink. I didn't think I could face life as it was. I couldn't face the truth of what I was. I couldn't face other people. But in the midst of that pain, I prayed for strength to get through it. It became the closest I had ever felt to God. As I look back, I realize how much God is with people in their suffering. I felt hopeless--absolutely hopeless. I knew I couldn't rely on myself. I knew that if I drank, I would die because I wouldn't be able to stop. The only option was God.

Sometimes in my life I have found that in order to truly experience God I have had to suffer. This suffering means not trying to change how I feel by simple means. On that day I realized that I didn't feel as though I fit in, I didn't want to go on with my life. And yet, it was at that point of extreme emotional pain that I felt close to God. I somehow knew that my feeling of desperation would not last forever, and I felt re-assured; the feeling did indeed pass. I felt God was telling me that I didn't have to numb my emotions with drink, drugs, sex—or even by pretending to be somebody else. It wasn't what I had to do. That's what I had done all my life. This was the beginning of my understanding of what it means to die to self. I began learning that when I don't rely on worldly things to change how I feel, I consistently feel a closer connection to God. Suffering of any form seems to take on a new meaning; it seems to become a means to know God. In a perverse way, it seems to be a joy when I realize that within that suffering I am being changed— corrected or loved—within it.

Over the years I have learned to be brutally honest with myself. I've learned how to be **appropriately** brutally honest, which is different from just brutal honesty.

One of my sisters came to faith on the back of the change in my life. She had issues of her own and she came to me because she saw that I had a peace I had not had before. She believed, but she still had massive issues within herself, within her life, with her self-esteem. She was a Christian, someone who was going to church, but still had this personal pain.

One day I took Dad to visit my sister and the three of us sat in the garden having a cup of coffee. My sister asked, "What do you think I need to do? There's something; I feel like I'm not giving myself all to God; that I'm holding back, but I don't know what to do."

I offered to pray for her and told her, "If we ask sincerely God will reveal what's in the way. But are you open to that? When it's revealed, you might not like it." I knew from experience when my truth was revealed I didn't like what I learned about myself.

She said, "Yes, pray for me." I put my hand on her shoulder and said, "Lord, anything that's in the way, let it be removed in the name of Jesus." I prayed as the Spirit led me for approximately twenty minutes when she experienced an obvious release from what had been binding her. She dissolved into tears and fell into Dad's arms and sobbed like a child. I prayed over both of them. I felt very grateful in my heart. I hadn't known what to pray for, but I felt as though the prayer had already been answered and I was flooded with gratitude in every part of me. The prayer was a prayer of thanksgiving.

From that point on my sister has been completely transformed. She knows peace like she has never known before. She is a teacher of four and five-year-old children and her teaching has been changed, she now teaches with the love of Christ, with a softness that replaced the fear that had been in her.

She recently told me she's no longer trying to fix herself. She feels God is doing a work in her. Because of the experiences she had she understands scripture in a more personal way, and it has become very real through the personal relationship she now has with Jesus.

This event had a profound effect on our father as well. Dad told me that if he told anyone about the experience, they wouldn't believe it. He said, "We've just witnessed a miracle." And then he added, "He's there for everybody Mick, isn't He?"

My sister now has a freedom which allows her to experience new, healthy relationships, not just with Jesus but also with other people.

Over the next seven years my dad and I became closer and closer as we learned to love and support each other. Dad's new understanding of addiction and homelessness transformed his faith; he began to understand the people that are suffering in a different way. We prayed together many times, and especially prayed for the people we saw on the streets. Dad asked me why he had not known years ago about the things he was learning now? Why had he not known about Jesus? Why had he never heard what it meant to belong to Jesus?

Dad told me that he believes that talking to a physically and/or mentally ill person on the street who may be hungry and spending all his/her money on drugs is where he sees Jesus. He didn't see Jesus in the church he had attended. Dad has been with me when I prayed with people and he witnessed the transformation that occurs when they accept Jesus. I also prayed for my dad when he was in pain and the pain left and he was able to walk freely. He experienced God's healing touch firsthand.

The freedom that God gave me as a result of my repentance affected Dad profoundly and our relationship brought Dad to understand and love in a new way. He experienced a strong loving relationship with Jesus and as a result began to enjoy a very close relationship with all his children and grandchildren. The changes in Dad profoundly impacted those around him, and he developed a humble innocence that came from the assurance that God is with him.

On another occasion, I visited Dad in the hospital. As I arrived, Dad asked me to pray for him. He then whispered to me, "Pray out loud because the man in the next bed needs to hear." I did as he asked and when I finished, I could see the peace on Dad's face. The man in the next bed who heard the prayer asked Dad if the praying made him feel any better. Dad replied that without prayer he was dead, but with prayer he was alive.

The man in the next bed asked me to pray for him and I did. This man had been resisting taking medication and had been argumentative with the nurses and others on the ward. After the prayer the man was silent which was out of character as he was normally constantly talking, sometimes erratically. But at this point he wasn't speaking at all.

Dad said to the other patient, "If you do as you are told in here, take your medicine, don't disrespect the other patients, don't disrespect the nurses, and thank God for your life, I'll guarantee you'll be out of here and back fishing within a month."

As soon as Dad said that the other man began to get really emotional and asked why no one has ever told him this before? It was like he understood something differently. I took hold of his hand and held it while the man cried.

The man changed his behavior and gratitude replaced his corrosive bitterness. He was looking at life in a different way. The man had previously not been able to get out of bed but when he started cooperating, within a day he was out of bed, like he believed he was going to be able to go fishing again. The nurses were laughing and wondering what had changed him. Dad shared Jesus with the man every day, he shared the peace one can have in a practical simple way.

Dad was looking back over his life as he approached ninety and saw where things were wrong and used his last years to speak out against injustice. He became obedient to Jesus. There was a voice he listened to, and it was not his own. I explained to him one day about the cross, the suffering love, and the endurance and what that means for a person, a human being, and he was profoundly affected. It was as though he understood the gospel in his heart, not just in his mind.

You cannot forgive yourself, only God can forgive you. But you must repent, and, in that action, God can work in your life and in the life of others. My pride falling in my act of repentance sorted out my life as well as my dad's life and the resulting relationship is one in which we both learned to hear what God is saying to us and to respond. Without repentance you can't be a Christian. To say you are sorry isn't enough; if you are truly repentant your pride will be torn apart. Dad was saved when he was eighty-seven, and at ninety he was a completely different man because his pride has been stripped away.

The kingdom of God is a world where we are free to be who God wants us to be and not a world where people tell us how to be. Pride and humility are opposites. Humility is what transforms.

I was clean and sober and trying to listen to God. I wasn't a part of a church fellowship, but I did have Christians advising and teaching me. In spite of my extensive criminal background, I began to help people who were struggling with addictions. These people were high profile addicts--well known to the police, hospital, drug and alcohol services--those seen as the hopeless cases. I initially worked with only one or two to help them get the things they needed—clothes, food, and other necessities. I prayed with them when they asked, and, as they became desperate in their life situations. Slowly but surely these people began to get clean and sober and their lives began to be noticeably different. The word spread as the people who knew each other and used drugs together started coming together and believing in God.

I received a phone call from drug services requesting that I meet with someone there. When I arrived, they asked me what

I was doing as they had been working with these people for ten to twelve years without a break-through. This took place in a small town with some hard-core addiction problems and the drug and alcohol workers as well as the police were beginning to see a difference; they wanted to know what was happening. They asked me if I needed any support for my efforts. I said, "No, not really," since I didn't think I needed anything. They asked me about the core of what I was doing; how are these people being changed? What is it you do? I replied, "I just ask God to make them better."

A short time later someone from a large Council housing[9] project called and asked to meet with me because a lot of the clients who lived in their houses and who had created problems resulting from drug and alcohol abuse had started to change. The social problems they had been experiencing were being transformed.

In our meeting they asked what I was doing. I told them I was just asking God to make them better. At the end of the meeting the administrators gave me a check for £1000. I didn't have any money of my own, I didn't know what to do with this money, but I knew that the £1000 was not for me. Instead I used it to help other people and for the first time in my life kept every receipt. I hadn't been sure I should have taken the money and so I felt I needed to be very accountable. Keeping every receipt was very much out of character for me.

[9] Houses or flats provided by the government at low rents for people who have low incomes

After a few weeks, probation services contacted me. They also requested a meeting and asked me the same kind of questions. They had been testing their clients for drugs and they were coming back clean--something unheard of. I told them the same thing: I simply asked God to help them and did what I could.

I began to feel prideful. I wasn't humble. I began to believe that I deserved the attention that I was receiving for helping others. It took away my insecurities and I began to feel confident and raise myself in my mind. I became proud.

At one point I was helping someone, and it was like I almost said in my mind, "It's okay, Jesus. I've got this one covered." I thought I was giving Jesus a rest and didn't realize my arrogance was growing stronger and stronger.

The environment where the alcoholics and addicts had been sitting on the street, drinking and doing drugs had changed by this time. One of the ladies I had helped had started going to a church and through her other addicts began finding their way to this same church. The people of the church and the pastor didn't not know how to cope with these newcomers and were unable to understand what was going on.

The pastor contacted me and asked to meet. I told the pastor about my own life and shared from an addiction perspective what had happened. The pastor looked me right in the eye, put his hands on my shoulders, and said, "But Mick, who is helping you?" I laughed because I didn't know what the pastor meant. I just laughed and said, "I don't need anybody; I'm all right." During this time, I prayed and believed, but there was a definite lack of humility in that belief.

I received a phone call from a female detective who asked me to come to the police station and talk with her. I asked what it was about, but she wouldn't tell me, so I said I wasn't coming. I immediately felt the old prejudice I had felt against police and my previous criminal mind behavior return—the "Who do they think they are?" attitude. The detective said if I didn't come in that they would arrest me and bring me in, but that they were asking me to come in voluntarily. I felt I needed to go.

I asked a free solicitor[10] to go with me since I had absolutely no idea why they wanted to see me. I assumed it was something from my past.

My solicitor and I went with the detectives into a tape-recorded interview where they asked me about the people I had been helping. They wanted to know how these people had gotten better. I was confused. I couldn't see where they were going; I thought they were looking for something criminal. I felt scared as I recalled my past experiences with the police. I asked if they could stop the interview, so I could pray. I just didn't know what to do. They stopped the interview; I silently prayed and asked God to speak as I didn't know what to do and was absolutely full of fear. They then carried on with the interview.

---

[10] A type of lawyer in Britain who is trained to prepare cases and give advice on legal subjects and can represent people in lower courts

The line of questioning was, "You prayed with people and they seemed to have gotten better, Is that right?" I said it was.

They asked what training I had, and what qualifications I had. I told them I didn't have any, that I didn't realize that I had to have any.

They asked, "What authority are you under? Are you under a church or what?" When the detective asked that question, I realized in my own mind that I was under my own authority and I immediately silently prayed for forgiveness. I physically felt the prayer leaving my body as I asked for forgiveness. I became very relaxed and warm, and I was able to speak very freely without fear.

They asked if I was some sort of leader of a group of people and I was able to say, "No, there are no leaders; we are just all servants." I found myself using scripture in everyday language—the words just flowed from me. As I looked back, I realized this was the Holy Spirit working through me.

They pulled out the photocopy of the £1000 check and their insinuation was that I had used deception in order to get the money. Thankfully, I had all the receipts in my car. Those receipts totaled more than £1000 and showed that I had spent the money on blankets, foods, pots and pans, and clothes to give to needy people.

The detectives wouldn't give up; they wanted an explanation of how peoples' lives had changed because of the prayers. They were adamant about demanding an explanation.

I told them, "I don't know. It's not me, it's God. I cannot make people better." As I said those words tears began to pour down my face and I realized what the real crime was; I had been claiming God's glory for myself. This was what I confessed to the detectives. "I think God's been helping these people and I have been trying to steal God's glory." I don't think they understood what I was saying. The detectives had a hardness about them; they had convicted me in their minds, and it appeared they would go to any lengths to find something to validate their belief. I knew they would find nothing.

The solicitor who was with me spoke up, laughingly. "So, can we just be clear? You are looking to charge this man because he prayed for people who were drinking, and they stopped drinking and got better? He's telling you he's a Christian and he believes in God and he believes God is doing for other people what they can't do for themselves. Please, will you charge him because I would love to take this to court?"

At that point the detectives stopped the tape. One detective, however, said off the tape, when we were alone, that she knew my police record from the past and she wouldn't rest until she found out what I was up to. I was able to walk away free and there were never any charges; it was finished with that conversation.

From that moment forward I understood I have no power on my own. If I ever get to a point where I feel my pride raising it's as if I feel a hand on my shoulder, telling me to sit down. It's a hand of love. It's as if Jesus is saying, "Sit down, Mick. I've got this one covered." Not the other way around. I learned that God works anyway--regardless of me.

I feel that it was my fear of being in trouble with the law that let me see the truth about myself. I felt that humility had been forced on me, and it was not something I chose. I learned, however, the importance of being under the authority of someone other than myself.   I learned that I must find some way to be accountable not only to God but also to someone else.   This was a huge lesson for me to learn.   I still find it difficult/painful, but I know that it is essential.

I am learning the difference between my will and God's, and it's my obedience to God's will that sets me free.   I've been given the ability to be grateful for the pain because in thanking God for the pain I learned what was wrong with me and how much God loves me.

This experience gave me a new understanding of suffering as well as a new understanding of the cross.   It seems that human nature is to ask God to take pain away, to remove anything that seems negative; but the way of God seems to be for us to be grateful for the new lessons learned in our pain.   I now understand this is the Kingdom of God at work in us.   It's very alien to be grateful for pain, but it is also very relevant.

One day I was praying and asking for guidance to grow spiritually; what would be meaningful for me?   What were the things I should do and should not do?   I asked God to show me a way forward.   While I was praying, I visualized a picture of myself made from glass and I could see everything inside of me. I was completely transparent, and everyone could see everything within me. They could see right through me. I heard the words, "This is how I want you to be."   That is not how I wanted to be! I didn't think I could be that transparent, I couldn't let people see how flawed I am, how weak I am—even my thoughts. I was afraid of what God was telling me He wanted me to be.

As the weeks passed and I continued to pray, I kept seeing myself as transparent with patches of darkness within me. I could see that image when I closed my eyes. Week after week. Then I began to see the darkness becoming lighter--from dark to gray, to lighter gray, to off white. The darkness was shrinking and getting smaller and smaller. As I prayed, I asked God to show me what I was doing that was right. I felt I was healing and getting better; I was certainly feeling better physically; I was reading the Bible more. The answer was, "You're not doing anything. I am." I was so relieved that all I had to do was to ask God what He wanted and then love and obey Him! Slowly but surely all this darkness would turn to light.

I still pray to be transparent and the darkness I now see in myself I can easily hand over to God. I no longer feel I need to hide; I have stopped hiding. I found that as I become more transparent many people who are dark inside have been drawn to me. I seem to be blessed as God shows me a way to help these people. I also find that many people I meet cannot be around me. They don't feel comfortable with what they can see in me. It used to be a lonely place until I realized that what they see in me is the love that they are seeking for themselves and I was once very much like they are now.

Being transparent means I don't have to defend or justify myself; it means I can be right or wrong. There are no gray areas. Sometimes people are drawn to me and I have been able to help them. But, as time goes on, many tend to turn away from God again in their actions. At this point they also don't want me to know what they are doing so they will either lie or not speak to me. For the most part these are people in recovery.

People are sometimes afraid of love and the possibility that reliance upon God is more powerful than reliance upon themselves. Instead of a willingness to be powerless they want to gain power, so they turn again to the things of the world for power. This is what happened to me when I was laying on the floor that Christmas Day after I was first sober. We think we can change ourselves by taking a drink or a drug or by finding a woman or denying the pain that we are in—we call upon the things of the world rather than calling upon the power of God that can truly get us through the suffering. When we call upon the things of the world, we are no longer transparent.

In suffering and in truth, we become more transparent. That concept draws some people, but it also scares some people away. The sorrow that I feel when people are no longer able to look at me or turn away from me for fear that I will judge them has helped me understand a bit of the sorrow God feels when we turn away from Him and reject the love and grace He freely wants to give to all who come to him. Knowing that I am a sinner, truly acknowledging my sin, and not being afraid to show how flawed I truly am, allows me to be free. When I pretend, to myself or the world around me that I am all right, and that I don't have any problems, then I too am turning away from God since I am not worshiping Him in the spirit of truth.

We all have a potential to turn to or to turn away from God. The pain seems to be in resisting and peace comes from turning to God. Sometimes suffering seems to cleanse, purify and rebuild a person. People have a natural reaction to not want to suffer so they tend to do anything, to say anything, to push it away, in order to avoid it. When you truly understand that it is Christ that is with you in the suffering you can truly understand, "Blessed are the poor in spirit" and it's all right to be who you truly are in Christ. You don't need to be anything else.

So, the lesson is that becoming transparent can be painful and human beings want to avoid pain. But when we acknowledge the pain, then we understand that Christ is with us in the pain and the pain becomes a joyful thing that draws us closer to Christ. This allows us to help other people.

I can't imagine a world where every human being would walk around completely transparent and everyone could see what the other person needs, and all freely give to each other. In the Kingdom of God there is no colour, and no creed--no one is any better than anyone else. We should all be transparent human beings, trying to reflect the light of Christ. Unless we are transparent how can the light shine out of us?

In September 2014 I gave a lift to a friend who had an appointment at Nazarene Theological College (NTC) in Didsbury, Manchester, England. As we walked onto the campus, we met the Registrar who asked me if I was interested in coming to study. I laughed because that seemed like a ridiculous idea—and I didn't even know the meaning of theology. When the Registrar explained it was the study of God—religion and faith-- I laughed even harder. I had little faith and was not prepared to study anything. The Registrar gave me a card with his name and phone number, saying he believed that I would come to NTC to study. After I left the campus the conversation remained in my mind and got stronger and stronger. I kept looking at the card and really wanted to tear it up but couldn't.

I was at my sister's house and told her about the incident on campus. I couldn't use a computer and even had difficulty reading. She looked up the college on the computer and asked, "Why don't you just call him? It can't hurt anything." Even though I was more afraid than I had ever been, I called and got an appointment. I met with representatives of the college and was offered a place to study.

At the same time, I received a job offer that was a dream job with a great salary, where I would be working in recovery. I was sure that I should take the job. It was irrational to even consider starting college at this time, and yet I had no peace about accepting that job. After struggling for some time, I made the decision to begin my course work at NTC and was filled with such peace that I knew I had made the right decision.

My first term in the fall went okay, and my grades were acceptable, but I had struggled and was aware that I could not read or write properly. As a result, I felt like I was pretending. Since I didn't know what to do, I just imitated what I saw other people doing and felt quite lost. I knew I could not continue that way.

About that time someone I trusted took the remainder of my grant money. Without money for rent I knew I would be homeless. I was, however, beginning to have a little bit of faith. I wasn't afraid to be homeless since I had been homeless before. I was sleeping in my car and had no money for food.

As I was praying in my car one evening, my phone rang, and it was the Principal of NTC. She asked, "Are you living in your car?" I had met her but didn't know her, so didn't quite know how to reply. I just said, "I might be." She told me to come to the college. I told her that I didn't know if I had enough petrol to get there. She replied, "You'll get here." And I did!

When I arrived on campus, I was given a key to a room with clean bedding and towels—and I could sense the love that filled the room. She left the room and returned with groceries. I was overwhelmed with the love I was being shown. For the first time in my life I really knew that I was not alone—even though no one was with me in the room. I couldn't understand the over-powering feeling that I was not alone.

Shortly after a floor collapsed at NTC and the repairs were going to cost thousands of pounds. The collapse took place during the holidays but since I lived there, I was aware of the problem and had extra time. People on campus had been so helpful to me and I wanted to give something back, so I offered to make the repairs. I was happy to have the opportunity to repay their kindness. NTC had no idea of my skill level and when they saw what I could do, they offered me a job to work for two days a week in exchange for rent. I felt valued and was thrilled to comply.

In the second semester I was trying to figure out what to do next. I had missed quite a few assignments while living in my car. I knew I would fail my first year. I thought I would just have to leave, find a job, and then carry on.

Without my looking for a job, one came up in recovery and I felt I should take it. However, while I was having coffee in the café with the HR Director, without my telling her anything about my personal life, she suddenly said to me, "It took me ten years to get my degree." I thought, "You know, I could probably do this if I prayed." So, I began praying-- realizing that in the past when I prayed it had worked. But I had prayed only when I was desperate: when things were going well, I neglected prayer. I told God that if this prayer for guidance worked that I would continue to pray all the time but if not, I would give up on prayer.

I was then offered a chance to repeat my first year of studies. The better paying job, however, was still waiting. As I prayed, I became convicted that I was to carry on with my studies. I knew I couldn't do it by myself, but I committed to carry on with what God had placed in my heart to do.

As I began my new academic year, the studies were going okay. In one of the courses, I was required to read an old classic Christian book of my choice. I chose John Wesley's **Christian Perfection**. As I read, even though the words were still mixed up, I felt a warmth from the book that I had never experienced. It was my first exposure to John Wesley, so I went to You Tube and watched an old video about Wesley's life. As I watched, I knew that something was missing in my own life. I believed in God, but I didn't have that "thing"—the "thing" I saw lived out in the Principal's life, the "thing" I saw in John Wesley's life—however, something was stirring inside me.

I went to the NTC Chaplain and told her that I didn't understand what was missing. I didn't know what it meant to be saved. When I had asked, no one could explain what it meant in a way that I could understand. People often used big words that I could not comprehend. The chaplain explained in simple terms what Jesus had done on the cross for us. I realized that Jesus wanted me to accept Him and as I did, I was broken. Until then I thought I had to do everything myself—I had to pray, I had to help people, and I had to do it all myself. When I realized that Jesus had already done it, and that it was Jesus all along, I was broken. Wesley had said he felt strangely warmed, and I now understood that since I too felt strangely warmed as I began to understand who Jesus is. I didn't need big words. I had met the person of Christ.

I passed the term and was pleased to be moving on to the second year of studies. I felt really alive! I recognized that I was not living under my own power but was living by the power of Jesus!

That summer I again worked with maintenance on campus. I was assigned to do a lot of painting and needed some help. I was feeling very close, very connected to God. I felt loved all the time.

One day a man walked onto the campus wearing painter's overalls. The man wasn't connected to NTC in any way. He walked up to reception and said, "I want to do some volunteer work, I am a painter." Within five minutes the man, whose name was David, was in the room with me.

I asked him how and why he had come. He said, "I came to speak to you. God's got something for you." I nearly fell off my ladder! David gave me a Kindle with a book about the Holy Spirit already on it. I read the book and began to understand the power of the Holy Spirit as I read. For the first time I prayed to the Holy Spirit and asked for a sign that I was doing the right thing. I didn't want to test God; I just wanted to be sure that it was God, since it was feeling a bit like magic and I needed assurance that it was indeed God.

The next morning as I walked into the kitchen, I rubbed my eyes, and couldn't believe what I was seeing—everything I looked at was illuminating rainbow colours! I could see the actual article, but every single image was shining like a rainbow. I was amazed! I went to the kitchen tap and was going to put water on my hands to wash my face. The water that came out was illuminated with rainbow colours! I washed my eyes and the colour became even sharper! I went to the door and as I looked outside each thing that I looked at was illuminated with this light. I came in and sat down and thanked God. After about fifteen minutes it was still there, and I still didn't understand what was happening. I didn't feel worthy of what I was seeing. I closed my eyes and asked God to help me understand what was happening. God spoke to me and said, "Now you know I am the light!" When I opened my eyes, everything was back to normal—but I knew my normal would never again be the same.

The next day David returned to help paint and we worked together for several days. As we talked, David told me to keep the Kindle. He asked me if I believed in angels. I said I did and then asked David why he had asked the question. David replied, "Why not?"

David was real—I introduced him to other people who also saw him and talked with him. But no one knew from where he had come or where he went. It has now been well over a year and no one knows anything else about him. No one even has a phone number for him. He just showed up to work and was assigned to work with me. God was at work in my life!

Even while a student I continued my personal ministry to the homeless and addicted. One night when I was working on the street, handing out food and clothes from the back of my car, a couple approached me and asked what I was doing. When I told them, they asked, "Why do you help these people?" I said, "Because I love them." They asked if I was a Christian and I said that I was. We chatted a bit and they asked for my phone number and then went on.

The next week I began to have serious problems with my car and had no idea where to get the money for repairs. There was also only one day left on my MOT[11]. I couldn't afford to pay for the MOT so would not be able to legally drive my car even if it was running. I was a bit overwhelmed. I stopped and prayed, just giving it all to God, acknowledging that I trusted His will for me and for my ministry. If God didn't provide the means for transport, I would accept that working from my car was not what God wanted me to do at this time. Regardless of the outcome, I was comfortable trusting God.

---

[11] Annual auto inspection in the UK

As I was praying my phone rang and the man I had met earlier on the street asked me to stop by his house after work. When I arrived, the man handed me an envelope containing cash and told me to buy a car. God had impressed upon the couple that they were to give this money in order for me to continue to work with the homeless. They knew nothing about me and had met me only the one time on the street. I bought a car and continued my ministry, giving God the glory.

In the fall of my second year at NTC I shared with the HR Director that I had trouble reading. She arranged for me to be tested and it was discovered that I have dyslexia. People with dyslexia benefit from special colour overlays or lenses tinted to correct their specific vision problems. I learned that if I could get these special tinted glasses, I would be able to read properly-- but the glasses were very expensive. I had no money so took the matter to the Lord in prayer.

Over a period of six weeks different people in different areas anonymously donated money at the Finance Office to help pay for the glasses. I personally told no one of my need. I was still £50 short when one of the NTC volunteers walked up and told me that he and his wife just wanted to bless me and handed me £50--completing the amount needed for the glasses. The first time I put the glasses on, my life was changed! I had never ever read a book all the way through and now I couldn't stop reading! I could see! Obviously, my grades improved--going from almost failing to a B+.

One of the biggest changes I noticed was that now when I read the Bible, I saw things differently. I could read not only the words but also the meaning and realized I had been literally blind. I was beginning to see things in the Bible that I never understood.

With the new term beginning I knew I needed books, but the ones I needed were very expensive. I had been praying about the finances and was quite concerned as I saw other students ordering them off the internet but had no idea how I would get the ones I needed. One morning I was sitting at McDonalds having a coffee and a man came in whom I recognized but couldn't recall from where. He came over and sat down across from me, shook my hand and asked if I remembered him. I confessed I did not. The man said that he worked for drug and alcohol services and I was the first person he worked with on his first hospital visit. He had assessed me more than seven years ago. He told me, "You were really poorly but now you look well. How are you doing and what are you doing?" I told him I was studying theology. The man smiled and said, "I have always prayed for you since I first met you because it was heartbreaking to see how ill you were." He told me he was a pastor and asked since I was studying if I needed any books? I assured him that I did! The pastor shared he had just cleared out a garage for someone from his church and the guy was a bit of an amateur theologian, so there was some good stuff in there. He invited me to come outside and look at the books in the boot[12] of his car. There were so many books that when we transferred them to my car, the books filled the boot, back seat and spilled onto the floor. Among them was every book I needed--and more!

---

[12] Trunk of car

I was living at the college and paying rent but as finances continued to be tight. I began asking God to guide me to accommodations that I could afford. I had paid for the next month but didn't know how I would pay from that point forward. I had been in prayer for about two weeks, asking God to show a way forward so I would know where to go. I felt I was supposed to be living somewhere else. I wasn't afraid but did feel that where I would go would not be in as comfortable as my present place and I hoped God would just send the money for me to stay at NTC.

One day I received a phone call from a pastor of a church where I sometimes attended, offering a flat at the church in exchange for a few tasks--mainly locking and unlocking from time to time. It would be rent free. I didn't have to think about it and instantly accepted the offer.

I then went to the college to tell them I would be leaving but was told that I had signed a contract for a full year and that if I left, I would still have to pay the balance of the contract. I left and went to the Lord in prayer, feeling something was not right. I went back to the Finance Office and asked if I could look at the contract I had signed. They couldn't find it. It seemed to have miraculously disappeared from the records. However, even though they couldn't find the written contract they felt they had a verbal contract. I told them the circumstances and that I felt God had called me to move forward to another place. I asked if they would help me do that. Within ten minutes permission was granted and I was cleared to move.

So, I had gone from not having a car, not being able to see, not having books, and not having a place to live—to receiving them all by the grace of God. It was through nothing I had done, other than trusting God to meet my needs, taking my needs to God and responding to God's leading.

I've learned from experience how greatly God can change lives--sometimes in an instant and sometimes over a course of time.

One day a friend that I had helped on the journey from addiction, called and said he was now working with another young man. The man calling was out of town but had been in contact with the young man over the internet. He learned the young man was planning to commit suicide. My friend said, "You believe in that Jesus—would you pray for him?" I said I would and asked for the address and phone number for the suicidal man. As I looked at the address, I realized that it was only about an hour away from me. I prayed, and instantly felt God telling me to go to the young man. I arrived and as I walked up to the house, I looked through a gap in the curtains and saw a young man standing on a chair with his head in a rope. I hurried to the front door, which was unlocked, and as I entered asked what he was doing. He told me he had been telling God he didn't want to do this and was asking God to help him. I told him Jesus had sent me. I helped him down from the chair and he broke down in tears in my arms. While I was praying with him, he was able to release to God some things that had happened to him in his past. I was able to stay in close touch with him and we were able to get him into rehab within two weeks. This highly intelligent young man's life was turned around and he is now studying for an advanced degree. Most importantly, he has returned to his faith!

From this experience I learned the importance of listening for God's voice and responding immediately. I have no justification for not obeying immediately when God speaks. As I started to pray with this mindset, God began using me in amazing ways to help others.

I had the opportunity to pray with another student at NTC who also had a troubled past. That student was experiencing absolute torment as he tried to hold on to control of his life and relationships, but he was at a breaking point. I knew I was to pray with him, so I made the offer and left it up to him. It was another two weeks before that student accepted my offer of prayer—when there was nothing left for him to try on his own. As I prayed with him, the man slipped into a semi-conscious state and began sobbing heavily. I prayed with him for about an hour and when he awoke, he was completely changed. He told me he had met with and surrendered to Jesus and knew he was no longer walking by himself. Since that time that student's life has been transformed, giving evidence of the power of his encounter with God.

Several years ago, I received a call from someone whom I had helped previously and who was now working in drug and alcohol services. The man was working with a lady who was very ill with addiction and such a mess that he didn't know what to do with her and wondered if I could help him. As we talked, I realized I was very close to their location. I went and spoke with them both. I had them come and sit in my car so we could talk privately. The lady was very ill; she was manic, couldn't be still. Heartbroken, unkempt, constantly crying, she was scattered, and her mind was running so fast that she was talking all over the place. She smelled strongly of alcohol.

I asked her what the real problem was. She told me her children had been removed from her home until they were eighteen, due to her drinking. She had been through court and the decision was final. She could have no contact with them. They were gone. I told her that wasn't the real problem. The real problem was that she hadn't asked Jesus to help her. The woman was desperate and asked, "Can I do it now?" She was very, very open and for a short time, I was able to pray with her and help her become calm: the manic behavior disappeared. In that moment she said, "Jesus, please help me." That's all she said. Nothing seemed to change.

We dropped her off at her home. The other man asked what her chances were. I replied that she was probably going to die and that her only chance was to turn to God. Otherwise there was no chance.

A month later the man rang me again and said, "You won't believe it but that woman you prayed with is not drinking. She has not had a drink since that day." She had gone to drug and alcohol services and they had scolded her for going through the rattle (alcohol withdrawal) without alcohol which can cause you to die unless you are on medication. She had not had a drink and had had no side effects. She was still in a desperate state mentally because she was starting to realize what she had done and how she had lost the children she loved. Within a week she was in rehab where she spent six months. In rehab she began to learn how to pray.

One night I was outside an AA meeting when a woman I didn't know approached me. I had no idea it was the same woman because she looked so different. She told me what had happened to her in the past six months. Although she looked very well, she said she still felt desperate and lost. She didn't seem to know how to live sober and alone. She asked me if I would take her through the twelve steps and as we completed those steps over the next three months, we became friends.

When you take someone through the twelve steps there is a complete confession process, an emptying-of-self process and the other person empties him/herself back. So basically, the two people involved know everything about each other since they are stripped bare of all secrets. After the process where she had learned I was a practicing Christian, she began to ask me questions about what it meant to follow Jesus. I told her that watching the Sermon on the Mount on YouTube had been the beginning of my life transformation. She began watching it and then I asked her to read the Gospel of John. After reading it she understood what was meant by light and dark. She caught onto what Jesus was in such a beautiful child-like way. It was humbling for me to hear the purity of her belief.

In all our time together, there had never been a male-female attraction. Our relationship felt holy, where each was treated with respect for who he/she was. As the friendship grew, she began to help me as I worked to help other people. I was able to direct women to her and she taught them to pray and become more confident in Christ.

One day she said to me that I seemed to pray with all these people and that they would get better. She knew that she had gotten better as well, but she still missed her children. I asked if she had prayed. She said she prayed for them every day. I asked, "But have you asked Jesus if you can have them back?" She had not. I asked why not. She responded, "I am afraid." I told her, "Ask Him now." As she prayed, the tears flowed.

Two weeks later I was at NTC just going into chapel when the phone rang. She said, "Mick, my babies are coming home!" The court had reversed the order and the children were being returned to her.

As our friendship grew there was still no attraction other than friendship. Once I took her with me to pray with a woman who wasn't well. Within that prayer we could feel the presence of the Holy Spirit and both women were in floods of tears. As the two women held each other they cried. It just felt perfect in every way. When I dropped her off at home, she said she felt as though something had been lifted from her and she felt even more peace than she had felt before.

As I put my arms around her to say a friendly goodnight, as I had done before, I felt something completely different that I had never felt before. I felt something from her and for her. I left knowing that I felt differently about her but wasn't sure how she felt. I knew that I couldn't pretend—I had spent my whole life pretending, and I knew I couldn't pretend. I called her that night and told her how I felt, and she said she felt the same way. I told her we need to meet next week and talk about our relationship. Her answer was, "No, we need to meet tomorrow and talk about it!

When we met, we decided we would start dating and see where it led. For the first time each of us made the decision that the relationship would be guided by prayer and we would see where God would take it. We both agreed there was something that wasn't of ourselves within the relationship and we wanted to give it a go.

We started spending more time together, helping other people and praying with other people. It seemed to just happen naturally. As Sarah watched me pray with people she knew, she saw the change that God made in people. She was struck by the miraculous power of Jesus that she was seeing right before her eyes.

Then she became very ill with a thyroid problem that resulted in a big lump on her neck. She developed extreme anxiety. She felt she couldn't go out--it was debilitating. We prayed about it together. We prayed that she would be able to cope and get through it. One day when she was very low and realized she couldn't physically leave the house, she rang and asked me to come and pray for her since she felt so desperate. On the forty-minute journey to be with her I asked the Lord if it was right to commit to this woman and give all of myself to her; if I was doing the right thing for both of us.

When I arrived, I asked what she wanted me to pray for and she said she said she wanted to be completely healed because she couldn't help anybody when she was like this. As I began to pray with her, I felt led to pray a deep meditative type of prayer. Halfway through the prayer I put two fingers of my right hand onto her throat and words just came to my mind. Aloud, I said, "Thank you!" The inside of her throat began to get hot--

first comfortably hot and then it got hotter and hotter. I continued praying uninterrupted for about an hour and as she opened her eyes it took her two to three minutes to be able to speak. She smiled and touched her throat; the lump had completely gone! Anxiety had completely left. None of it has returned. She has been free since that day. She had been diagnosed with Grey's Disease, but that diagnosis has been reversed. She is now able to go into public without any anxiety.

At the moment she was healed I knew that she was the woman God had planned for me. I went to her mother and father and asked for permission to marry her and both said yes. Days later I asked her to marry me and she accepted. Because of finances we had no ring but neither minded. However, I had been praying for a ring since I wanted her to feel comfortable and to know that it was real. I went to tell one of my sisters that I had gotten engaged and her first words were, "Do you have a ring?" I replied that I did not. She went upstairs and came down with a beautiful ring which she gave to me. I thanked God for it, prayed over it, and then took it and put it on Sarah's finger. It fit perfectly!

The fact that we had already dealt with all the things in our past and that God had dealt with those things provided a complete freedom in our relationship. We have no secrets-- nothing we fear the other will find out about us. We are letting God decide the wedding date. We feel that everything has happened so naturally that we want Him to decide the speed at which we are to go and where we are not to go. God is doing all the work.

PART TWO

Miracles

I want to give glory to God for the way He works in and through me, but I do not always know how to share the way God has used me in the lives of others. My father who had witnessed some of these things with me said, "If you told someone they wouldn't believe it. You have to be there." This book is being shared to give God glory.

I pray for God to use me and to let me see opportunities to serve, and God responds. We want God to use us in a way we understand but God uses us in ways we may never understand. Our job is just to obey. I do share with the people who have provided the resources I use as I feel it is important for them to know how God is working. That's how God works; He uses us all together to accomplish His plan and His purpose. The following incidents are just some of the ways God has worked in and through me.

I received a phone call from a lady who believed that she had some kind of demonic influence over her. She was a stable woman in every respect and had no mental health issues. She wasn't a believer but had some idea of spirituality. She had traveled to South America approximately four months before she called. While there she participated in some type of religious ceremony where she drank ayahuasca, a highly hallucinogenic drug which is supposed to give people a "god experience".

When we met, I asked why she had called. She said when she was talking to her boyfriend's nephew, he casually said something about Jesus. She immediately spat at him and attacked him and had to be physically dragged off him. She knew what she was doing but it wasn't her; she couldn't stop it and she didn't know why she was doing it. When she was talking with me, she couldn't say the name of Jesus but could say "the so-called Son of God." She couldn't speak the name of Jesus out loud. I asked what she thought I could do. She said, "I think you know Him. Just help me."

There were four other people in the house when I arrived, nice gentlemen with some kind of spirituality. They were looking at me to see what was going to happen--looking for some kind of spiritual experience. Her friends were in the kitchen, so I took her into the next room and partially closed the door and began to pray.

As I prayed her eyes began to close, her head tilted back, her eyes rolled back, and her eyes began to flicker. Every time I said the word "Jesus", she got more and more agitated. Within five minutes of praying for her I asked, "With whom am I speaking?" She said, "The one whose real name is Light." I continued praying and said, "There is only one light and that light is Jesus." Her voice became deeper and growling like from her throat. I put two fingers on the side of her throat and said, "Quiet! Peace, in the name of Jesus." She stopped speaking and seemed to relax.

I left her sitting and went into the kitchen and asked the men as a group if they could pray in the name of Jesus and they nodded yes. I then asked that same question to each

71

one individually. Each one nodded and said yes. We all went back into the other room and they put their hands on each of her shoulders. I told them they could pray silently or out loud, but it had to be in the name of Jesus. I continued to pray aloud and as we were praying, calmness fell over the room, a happy calmness, a peace that was not there before. There was a high pitch buzzing sound that stayed in the room. As I prayed and felt this peace, I said, "Leave, in the name of Jesus Christ." And everyone in the room began to pray and everyone began to sob and sob.

I asked them to remove their hands from her shoulders. I then took her in my arms as though she were a small child and she cried and cried. I whispered in her ear and asked if someone had hurt her when she was a little girl. She was shocked and said, "How did you know?" I let her know that Jesus told me, and that Jesus loves her. Without further speaking everyone put their arms around each other and wept tears of joy and peace. I prayed a prayer of thanksgiving and as we finished praying, she looked different. One of the guys said, "What's happened to her? Her eyes look different." I said, "I think she's found Him."

She said, "I feel different. What do I need to do?" I told her to pray only in the name of Jesus. I also told her to remove anything from the house that was linked to other means of spirituality—crystals, Buddha, and objects that spoke of other types of spirituality. I told her to get rid of all of them and pray only in the name of Jesus. I had a Gospel of John and gave it to her, suggesting she read the book so that she could see who just saved her and why.

Two of the men in the house seemed to be more profoundly affected by what happened than the other two and asked me to pray for them. They each accepted Christ. They asked to be baptized and are receiving instruction on what it means to be a Christian.

A week later I received a phone call from the same lady. She said her boyfriend's friend was spiritually unwell--almost to a demonic point and would it be possible for her to take me to see him. I agreed. My finance Sarah, the lady, her boyfriend, the friend, and I met together. As I spoke to the young man, who was about thirty, it seemed highly likely that he had mental health issues. It appeared he was suffering from drug induced psychosis. He was talking about Jesus, but it wasn't in a biblical context. He wasn't preaching the gospel. He was preaching a different message than the gospel. He believed he could see demons physically and he most certainly was a tortured human being both mentally and physically. I could see and hear it.

I let him speak for about ten minutes during which time he spoke very fast, going from one subject to another, very erratically. Everyone was quiet, listening to what he had to say. I asked him to stop for a second. Then I asked the young man, "Why am I here, and what have I come for?" He answered, "Because you can see what I can see." I asked if I could pray for him and he said yes.

I put my hand on the man's shoulder and began to pray and asked for peace to fall and for anything that was in the way of truth to be removed. As I prayed the young man began to shake physically and then began to cry. At this point I took Sarah's hand and put it on the man's shoulder and asked her to pray aloud. As she prayed, the young man fell to his knees and she bent down to her knees and held him like a child. They cried together as I prayed with one hand on each of their shoulders.

As we all sat back down, I asked him what he thought God was trying to say to him and what he thought he should do. He said, "I can't smoke weed and follow Jesus. I'll never smoke it again. I've been ill, I just didn't know." He was talking slowly and speaking coherently, and he looked physically different. He had a Bible with him, and I opened it to the book of John and advised him that it would be a good book to read that evening.

The woman rang me three days later and said her boyfriend asked her to call to see if I would come and pray with him. Sarah and I went to the house. I began by asking the man how he felt. He said he felt frightened. I asked him why he felt frightened and he said, "Because I have seen the power of God working." I told him, "That's a good thing!" I asked him why I was there. And he said, "To pray for me." I asked what I should pray for. He said he had been really, really shocked when his girlfriend had spit at his nephew when he said the name of Jesus. It had really scared him, and he was full of fear.

I somehow sensed that the man had seen something like that before; I strongly felt that he had, but that he hadn't spoken about it. The man said he had. He told us his former girlfriend had tried to attack him and all he had done was casually mention the name of Jesus. She immediately attacked him and was spitting at him. He had to pin her down as she was cursing at him. I could see that his current girlfriend didn't like what she was hearing; I saw her getting tense and agitated. I asked if I could pray. I began to pray for all in the room. The prayer included the statement that when we sleep with people, we give up part of ourselves and we open ourselves up to a spirituality that can either be good or bad. Within the prayer I explained that the feelings of jealously, envy, possession, and love, were all mixed together. Something changed within the four of is. It was for all of us, as we all identified with that prayer. A peace again fell on the room, and a buzzing noise came upon the room which we all heard, like a white noise.

I prayed again, asking for forgiveness for each of us, for things that had gone wrong in past relationships. Everyone in the room was reduced to tears; it was a highly emotional atmosphere. I then asked the man what had changed. He said, "Everything." Sarah and I left. Later I saw the man outside a drug rehabilitation program meeting. He was clean and abstinent of drugs. I didn't even know that he had been using drugs but learned that after 15 years of drugs, he was now abstinent.

I was called to see a lady who was suffering with alcoholism, drug addiction, bulimia, and self-harming; she was very ill. As I normally do when calling on a single woman, I took Sarah with me for the visit. I asked her if she needed medical or mental health help. It was obvious that she did, but I wanted her to acknowledge her need. She said she did need help but been told by health services that she wasn't ill enough, no beds were available.

The crisis team she had contacted told her to listen to music, and to go on walks—none of which she could do because she was too ill--and her mind was going too fast. She told us she was constantly going from one room to the other because she couldn't stay still, and she couldn't rest. Her thoughts were constantly telling her that she needed to kill herself. There were no voices--just the constant thought that she needed to kill herself.

I asked what we should pray for her. I told her that when we prayed with people something always happened, either while we were there or after and asked if she was okay for things to change for her. She said, "Yes, I'm just desperate."

I began to pray and as I was praying, I asked for peace to fall and, as often seems to happen, there was something like a white noise, a ringing in our ears, which we all experienced. I began to pray that first she would feel forgiven for anything she had done. I could see that she was nodding her head in agreement with her eyes closed. At that point I felt convicted to say, "I am going to pray for you as an innocent little girl so that you can forgive those who hurt you." Within a couple of seconds, she began to weep and sob. At that point Sarah went and sat next to her and held her. I continued praying and asking for forgiveness—for all the people in the room and for all the people who had harmed them. At that point the prayer became about all of us. We were all in tears at this point. Sarah was holding the lady and I prayed over both for healing. The two women just rocked each other and cried together. The lady said, "How did you know that he abused me? I've never told anybody." I replied, "I didn't, but Jesus does, and He loves you."

I fell to my knees in front of them both and asked them both to pray for me. They each put a hand on my shoulders and prayed a prayer of thanksgiving and protection. When they finished the three of us just held each other; the feeling was that in the process we had become equal--all one. After we finished praying, the lady said, "Why do I feel this peace? I've never felt like this in my life. What is it?" I told her she was feeling Jesus, God, the Holy Spirit. She said, "I just feel like I want to tell everybody and shout it out."

I gave her a Gospel of John and told her reading it would help her to understand what was happening to her and what had happened for her. When we left, she was a different person, she was calm and at peace and without agitation. The next day she messaged me with a photograph of her hand holding the Gospel of John. Out of the blue a bed had become available and she was going to get some psychiatric help. She was taking the gospel with her. The words underneath the photo simply said, "Thank you."

A few days later I received a call from a desperate lady. Her father had recently died, and she was drinking heavily. She had just been suspended from her job due to her alcoholism, and she could not stop drinking.

Sarah and I went to see her. She was very, very erratic-- not drunk, but talking quickly and going from one subject to another. She couldn't even look at me and acknowledged, "I don't know what's the matter with me. I can't even look at you!"

The lady had been brought up with a strong Catholic tradition. When I asked her if we should pray, she wanted to pray the Lord 's Prayer and the Hail Mary, which she did. When she stopped, she said she felt like God wasn't listening to her prayers.

I suggested that we pray for her to receive forgiveness. She said she couldn't be forgiven because of the bad things she had done. I told her that's why Jesus came. The three of us prayed that she would receive God's forgiveness. I asked her if she could forgive the people who had hurt her. She said she didn't think she could unless she got a sign from God.

She was sitting next to the fireplace and she got up to get a photograph of her father who had recently passed away. In the process, something fell into the glass of wine she was drinking. We thought it was a penny, since we knew it was something metal, but when she picked the glass up, it was a small crucifix that had fallen into the bottom of the glass of wine. She became very emotional and said, "Jesus is with me at the bottom of the glass." Then she told us that she had been sexually abused as a child and she didn't know if she could forgive the man. I told her she didn't have to forgive but was she willing to forgive?   She said, "Yes, I am willing."

I put my hand on her head and prayed for the Holy Spirit to fill her, for forgiveness to flow through her body, and for her to know and feel the true forgiveness of Christ. She gave a deep sigh; a sound of pleasurable release came from within her. She sat back in the chair, relaxed. No agitation, just completely relaxed. At that point I told her it was time for us to go and for her to just spend time in the presence of God. Then we left.

Eight hours later I received a message from her saying thank you and that she hadn't had a drink since. This would have been impossible without the help of the Holy Spirit.

During the next three months Sarah and I were led to women who were suffering from past issues and needed to be brought together. When I was praying, I felt that Sarah should meet with these women for a prayer group which would be Christ-centred, where they would all be equal and support each other in prayer. I met with the group for the first time so I could help them understand that they were coming together equally in Christ and that Christ was the true leader of the group.

Through many experiences working with others I have gained a new realization that in the sexual act, whether forced or consensual, something happens; there is a spiritual element to it that affects those involved in either a positive or negative way. I have a new understanding of the importance of marriage and the coming together, two as one, as God intended. I have seen a great number of people who were abused as children. I have also observed that when the sexual act is twisted whether by abuse or through multiple partners there is a powerful negative impact on people in their lives and relationships. It seems to have a dark spiritual hold over people, which causes a negative self-image that is in no way Christ-like. I speak from personal experience and know that with God's help I have broken free from that myself.

I was helping a man get off drugs and alcohol. I would go around to his house, listen to him, and pray with him. Even though he wasn't a Christian, he wanted me to pray for him as he said when we prayed, he felt a peace and thought with prayer he would be able to stay sober. When he had been sober for about eight weeks, he began to ask me

questions about faith, about this "Jesus thing", about God.   I
tried to explain the gospel to him in very simple terms.   I
prayed that God would show Himself to the man in a way that
the man would understand.

When we finished praying, the man's nine-year-old son
came into the room. The son has mild autism, is ADHD, and
is a troubled young man who swears excessively. He doesn't
have a mum in his life, his dad takes care of him. The boy
asked, "What are you doing? Are you talking to Jesus?" and
I replied that we were. The boy said, "I would stab Jesus up."
I was shocked! His dad was about to tell him off, but I
stopped him and said, "No, it's okay."

I asked the boy if he wanted to sit down with us and the
boy came and sat down. He asked, "What would Jesus do if
I stabbed him up? What would He do to me?" I told him,
"He'd tell you He loved you." The boy replied, "I would chop
His arms off then. What would Jesus do to me then?" I
replied, "He'd tell you He loved you even more."

The boy stopped, was quiet for a minute, and then he
said, "My dad's like Jesus because when I hurt him, he loves
me. So, I love Jesus." Then the boy got up and went out to
play.

His father broke down in tears and he accepted Christ at
that moment. He understood the gospel because it came
from a child.   When his child had talked about hurting Jesus
but realized there was still love, the father understood that
though he was full of sin, God still loved him. It was in
recognizing God's love for him in spite of his sin, that he was
able to accept Christ. The change in the father has been

miraculous and although the child is still problematic there is a strong love between them. They seemed to realize how much they need each other, and they pray together as well.

I came to understand that it's important to listen. It's important not to dismiss people: children, alcoholics, drug addicts, anyone. It's very, very important to listen to everybody. God seems to speak so powerfully through innocence. So powerfully--sometimes through people we think don't know Him.

Sarah received a phone call from a lady asking me to come and pray for a woman who was struggling with alcohol. She said the woman is a devout Christian, knows the Bible back to front, and all that. Sarah said she would ask me. Then the lady said she had heard that I prayed with people and then they got better. She said, "She wanted Mick Fleming to pray for her and it was only him that could help her." When I heard this, I felt sick. I felt sick to my core! I asked the Lord to forgive me if I had ever led anyone to believe that I was the power. I prayed for the woman to see real truth. I prayed for guidance in this situation. I then called the woman back and told her that it would be a good idea for me to pray with her over the phone. I explained that it is God that does the work, and if she and I prayed together over the phone, she could then go to her alcoholic friend and pray with her. God would be present, and I didn't need to be there. I asked her to explain to the lady that I couldn't come and pray for her when she thought the power was coming from me. If God willed it, I was sure we would meet another time under different circumstances.

Because of my past experiences I feel like the Holy Spirit tells me when to stay and when to go, as well as when to avoid stepping into someone else's sin. It's become clear how to be loving and caring without stepping into the situation.

I have learned that when one goes against the Holy Spirit it sometimes deprives another person of helping and it can sometimes stop the person who needs the help from getting the help he/she needs. I know I have no power. I must say yes or no to the Holy Spirit. There is nothing in between. That has become blatantly clear to me. I instinctively know how to respond and when not to respond as well. In a split second, the questions come, "Am I helping this person for my own glory? Can I help this person? Is it appropriate?" and I know—I get the answer straight away. I am then faced with a free will choice. Do I go or not? I seem comfortable knowing when I'm not to go, when the situation is not quite right, when God doesn't want me to go. But knowing when to go—I know when I should go, but sometimes don't. Sometimes through my own pride or fear I hold back. Thankfully those times come less and less.

As part of a Social Justice course I went with my class in the evening to Manchester City Centre where the mayor was speaking about homelessness and how the Christian community could be involved. As we came out and were waiting for a taxi, a couple of homeless people walked past. I stood back and watched as some of my classmates were asked if they had any change. Most said no, but I watched one man respond by passing some money through a handshake and not drawing attention to himself. When the next homeless man came and requested change, even the man who had just given the money said, "No."

When the next homeless man came by, I felt the Lord saying, "Now go." I didn't want to go because I felt uncomfortable going in front of my classmates and the other people around me. But I said, "Your will be done," and went straight away. I made eye contact with the man, put my hand out and we shook hands. I said, "Come inside." The man came inside with me. I asked his name and had a ten-minute conversation with him, found out about his life. He had a daughter; he used a lot of drugs but in his mind, he wasn't an addict. I asked him if he would answer one question; "Don't tell me what you want, but please tell me what you need." The man replied, "I just need someone to care about me." I put my arms around him, and the man cried and cried. I asked why he was crying. He said, "Because you spoke to me and called me by my name. Nobody ever calls me by my name." I asked him if he thought his life could change and he said, "I pray it can." I asked the man if he believed in God. He said, "I have to, because I have nowhere else to turn." I asked if I could pray for him and he agreed. I prayed for him, gave him a Gospel of John, and put some change in his hand. Then the man asked if he could pray for me. The man prayed for me and then said, "We are brothers now." The taxi had arrived, and someone came in to get me. As the two of us embraced in parting, it felt that we had become brothers...family. I could easily not have responded, but by responding I met my brother.

In all the years that I have asked, "Tell me what you need, not what you want," I've never had someone say money, even when they had a sign asking for money. This tells me the spiritual need is much greater than the material needs. Asking them what they need, out of respect and love, is so important. They must search deeper to consider what they need, and it's never money.

I went to see an old friend; someone not of faith; someone that lives in a very poor neighbourhood. I was welcomed with open arms, given coffee, and made to feel very welcome in my friend's home. As we were talking, a knock came to the door and my friend invited the man at the door to come in. The man brought in some steaks, chicken, big jars of coffee. My friend bought it all. Then he called his young son in and said take the meat next door, the coffee across the road, and then just carried on talking with me as though nothing out of the ordinary had happened. I realized that for him, this was ordinary. Within a half an hour there was another knock at the door, and it was someone who was returning a pouch of tobacco that he had borrowed. Within twenty minutes a lady knocked and walked into the house with a bag of potatoes and a bottle of milk which she gave him and then left. I asked him what was happening with all the people coming to his house. He replied, "We look after each other Mick. We all look after each other. None of us go hungry. We never go without a fag[13]." I felt my friend was struggling with how he was living, struggling with faith, and I pray he finds it.

I was reminded of the parable Jesus told in Luke 16 about the man who excused half of the debt of those who owed his master. His master admired the dishonest rascal for being so shrewd and it is true that the children of this world are shrewder in dealing with the world around them than are the children of the light. I thought about how it was all of them coming together to help each other. They were all equal in the transactions; there wasn't one above the other.

I believe the church could learn so much through their interaction. Where are we equal, where are we beneficial to one another without a second thought? Being so natural in our care of each other that equality is a normal way of life? For me, the lesson and example of God came from a deprived community that loved each other in the only way they knew how. I knew some of the things going on in the

---

[13] Cigarette

neighbourhood were wrong, and I would not have participated, but I felt no need to make judgement—I left that to God. I could see God working in that neighbourhood. It struck me how easily the scripture came to mind to fit the situation so perfectly and how alive scripture is in the world we live in if we will only look. In the parable told in Luke the master was happy, so leaving what is sinful and what is not up to God seems right. I am not wanting to justify sin in any way but being aware that God works whether people believe in Him or not. Believers should take notice. Sometimes we see a certain type of lifestyle and assume there is no God in it but when we spend time with the people involved, we see God. Sometimes communities of poverty can be close to the truth of who and what God is, even though they may not realize it.

These people were aware that if they needed anything they could just go to the door and knock. It would always be open, never be closed. There was no pride involved. This is a powerful lesson and reminder that when we knock on God's door it will always be opened and He will provide whatever we need.

It makes one not judge, even though you recognize sin, it's important to let God be the judge for it's to Him that they are accountable. And God asks, "Why are you not coming? Why are you not giving?"

I received a call from a lady who had been referred by a person I had prayed for a couple of years ago. She asked if I would come and pray for her. I asked her what she wanted prayer for. She told me she had MS and was desperately seeking some sort of freedom. I told her I am a Christian and if I did pray for her, I would be praying in the name of Jesus. She was a bit reluctant, she said she didn't think she wanted to become a Christian and she didn't think she ever would. She told me she practiced Shamanism[14]. I said that I understood, but I could only pray in the name of Jesus and nothing else and understood if she didn't want me to come pray with her. She chose to think about it.

She called me back a day later and said she felt so desperate that would I please come pray for her; she didn't mind if I prayed in the name of Jesus. When I learned she lived alone I asked if it was okay if I brought my finance with me as it would be more appropriate and, as a Christian, she would pray with us. She agreed.

When she told me where she lived, I found it remarkable that it was just around the corner from the college where I was studying. The person who referred her lives over 300 miles away. Didsbury is a small place and yet there was no other connection between us, so I felt encouraged.   In preparation for the visit I asked a few other people to pray for us as we went.

On the night we went to see the lady when she answered the door she was stooped over, with shoulders rounded

---

[14] Eastern spirituality

down, shuffling, and could hardly walk. When we entered the living room it was filled with all types of imagines of Eastern religions, ornaments on the wall, Buddhism, Hinduism, Shamanism. Every religion seemed to be represented except any symbol of Christ.

As we sat, she began to speak, and she was speaking very quickly. Her mind was quite erratic, and she moved quickly from one subject to another. It seemed obvious that there was a spiritual element to her illness. She talked constantly, non-stop, for about fifteen minutes and then I asked her to stop. I asked her to please listen because what I had to say might change her life. I explained the gospel to her in a very simple way. I said, "If you confess everything you have ever done wrong, God will forgive you and take that sin away. And the sin of everything that has been done to you will be taken away as well and you will step into a new life and into a new world of love and peace. This is the understanding of Jesus' life, death, and resurrection. Do you want me to pray with you now?" She replied that she did.

I prayed, asking the Lord for the lady to have the strength to confess everything and that He would hear our prayers as we all came together as one. As I was praying the woman began to spew out everything from being a child to a grown woman, everything she had done wrong. There was no thought in it, it just poured out. It went on and on and on for almost half an hour. As she was speaking the words started to become somewhat blurred—this deep-rooted confession that she seemed to have no control over began to sound gibberish—the words made no sense in the end. At that point, I put my hands on her shoulders and asked the Lord to show this woman that she was forgiven and loved by Him. She began to cry and continued to sob. Sarah sat next to her and put her arms around her and as I prayed the two women cried together and held each other. There was probably another half hour of praying and tears. As the lady lifted her head her eyes looked completely different. She immediately stood up and started moving her legs, she said, as she had never been able to move them before. She stood upright, no longer round shouldered and hunched. She was ecstatic and full of joy.

She asked, "Can I pray for you two?" We agreed, and she prayed a prayer of gratitude for us coming and for the healing she believed she had received. Remarkably, at the end of the prayer she said, "In Jesus' name." Sarah will continue contact with her, will befriend her, and these two ladies will pray together and teach each other the love of Christ. There is no expectation of anything. The result will be in the hands of the Lord.

As we were driving home, I was feeling genuinely in awe of God, thanking God for what He had done but I also knew I was feeling prideful. I felt powerful and I knew that was wrong. Even as I was praying for God to take the pride away, a part of me still wanted to keep it. I had to battle for several days before I was eventually able to give it all over to God. It's one thing to know in your mind that it is God. But it is very dangerous to try to steal God's glory. That's something I must constantly battle, and I need the prayers of others to help me remember that the power is totally God's and that I am merely an instrument. I have been blessed to see many, many miraculous things in the time I have been a Christian but the biggest blessing of all is that God shows me how to let go of my own sin within that process. Even though I knew the truth, a part of me wanted to steal the glory from God and I had difficulty stopping myself. This helps me realize I am still a sinner and need God's forgiveness as much as anyone else. I know that if any of us take credit for what we have done, it is pride, which is a sin. We need to confess it, repent and give all the glory to God. It is only the ability to identify sin in ourselves that allows us to do that. I really wanted to bask in the glory of what had happened, but I knew it was a sin. It humbles me to see the miracles, but it may also take a bit of time for me to recognize and confess in my heart that I am feeling prideful and give the glory completely to God. Every Christian has the ability within him/her to recognize his/her own sin, give it to God, and to be free. I had to go through the same process after the healing as the lady went through to be healed; I, too, had to lay my sin down before God so that I could be healed from my pride.

We need to be grateful when the Holy Spirit convicts us of our own sin so that we can repent and be forgiven to continue in a transparent relationship with God. This is key to the gospel.

Through the years I have become aware of the gospel being spread around me. As I have helped others recover from their addiction and come to faith in Christ, I have witnessed those people reaching out to others and leading them to faith. I watched the network around me growing bigger and bigger as people come to faith in Christ from their broken beginning. I was reminded of this by two men that I had been working with over a period of about three months. They came to faith by reading the Gospel of John, asking questions, and accepting Christ. They in turn went out to help others who were suffering. I feel there is something so powerful about the gospel when it is preached to the poor— whether they are spiritually poor or materially poor. My experience is that the comfortable person rejects the gospel much easier because they don't feel there's a need for change.

I am very much reminded of when Paul went to Jerusalem to see Peter, James and John, as described in Galatians. They shake his hand and confirm that he is to preach the gospel to the gentiles. But almost as a throw away comment at the end of the conversation they say, "Don't forget the poor." I feel like the gospel and the poor are entwined. Also in Galatians, as Paul went to see the apostles and they shake his right hand in front of witnesses, which in those days would have made it a legally binding contract, saying if you are going to preach the gospel, then you can't forget the poor.

It brings the need for soup and evangelism to be offered together. They are inseparable, they are part of the same thing. Just to stand up and preach, whether in church or on the street, to people who are starving is not enough. All their needs must be met, including spiritual, physical and emotional needs. And that means a time commitment beyond just the preaching. When sharing the gospel, we are sharing Christ and He is far more than just words.

Watching the gospel transform people in my own life and ministry takes on a shape and a form that has nothing to do with me. This has caused my faith in God to grow. I know it is not me or any other human that is making things happen— it is the Holy Spirit.

I advise people who are working with non-believers to focus on maybe two people at a time so that he/she will be mindful of his/her own health and spiritual wellbeing. It is important to let God do the leading and not try to do things in one's own power. It's not a cut-off point, it's a matter of discernment. The need is great but allow the Holy Spirit to lead in your service. People who are just recovering have a great zeal to spread the gospel and help people. But there can be such a powerful feeling after helping people that pride can come in and one may begin to forget that it's the Holy Spirit that has the power and not the person being used. This can be a downfall for any of us, but particularly for those with an addictive nature, as the power can become another kind of addiction. It's important as we mentor to remind others where the power comes from and remember that without Christ, we can do nothing. Just another reason why we need to be together in ministry. When one helps someone, that person, in turn, will allow the helper to point an error out without feeling defensive. Correction is more easily accepted from those who are closest to us and who have helped us to grow. It's very important that we encourage each other and build each other up in the truth.

I was asked to speak at a soup kitchen and, after speaking, was sitting to eat with the people. I was drawn to a man who had been shouting out when I was talking. Even when I was speaking, I felt drawn to the man, as though he were the only one in the room. It turns out that the man was an alcoholic, a bit of a character, who was well known to the others. I spoke with him for at least an hour, got to know about his children, his past, his abuse. The man shared deeply.

As we were talking, people came around giving tracts and those eating would take them and then toss them aside. I realized that the way they were trying to evangelize wasn't working. The man I was visiting with took one, wadded it up and tossed it aside.

I thought it might be better to just speak to him in the truth. I asked him, "Are you ready to die?" It wasn't what I intended to say—it just came out; I couldn't stop it coming out. The man looked right into my eyes, took hold of my hand and started to cry. He said, "I'm dying and I'm afraid; I'm scared. I've done lots of bad things." I asked if he wanted to tell God about them. I told him, "You don't have to even say them out loud. You can either whisper them in my ear or just tell God in your mind. You can get relief from this burden and you don't have to be afraid anymore." So, we prayed together. He accepted the Lord and the tears he was crying with fear turned to joy right before my eyes as we hugged each other. We parted as friends...as brothers. One meets a stranger and he/she becomes a genuine brother or sister, and that's how we parted.

Within a week I found out from the man's brother that he had passed quietly in his sleep, but I am sure he was not afraid. I felt upset that he died because I thought maybe God had wonderful plans for the man. I wasn't angry at God but was a bit despondent. I told someone else how I was feeling, and the friend replied, "Maybe God did have plans for him. He sent you, so He could take him home." Then I understood again the real importance of being obedient, of taking time to care. We really don't know what's going to happen in another's life.

I met a man who had a house but was spending time on the street because he was lonely. He was profoundly alcoholic. He had been a very successful businessman, but he had lost everything—his wife, his children. He talked as though he still had all those things. He had an alcoholic arrogance. I spent a lot of time with him. We would meet for coffee and talk. He was still drinking but he had moments of clarity. He was a nice man, but he was suffering from the illness of alcoholism. One day he said, "What do I need to do? Why can I not stop? Show me what I need to do. Help me!" I told him that only God could help him with his alcoholism. I could only suggest things, but I have no power to help him, it is only God's power that can help him. The man asked me if I would pray for him and I did. As we were praying the man fell to his knees in prayer. I didn't ask him to confess any sins, I just prayed that God would release him. After we prayed, the man confessed some horrendous things and asked, "Can He even forgive me?" I told him, "Especially you!" Jesus said He came to relieve people from all sins. The man broke down and cried and then accepted the Lord.

He did become a better man, but he didn't stop drinking. The last conversation I had with him, we had had a coffee, and were in my car. We prayed together, and I sensed God was giving the man a choice.

I told him, "You've got a choice. You know what God wants you to do and you need His power to carry it out. You've got to stop, mate, or it will be too late." The man said, "I don't understand. I don't." We were in the car and drove to a McDonald's car park and I said, "Take a look at that McDonald's. You don't bring your children here." I drove from there straight to the Emergency and Accident Unit because this was where the man had been over 100 times in that year when he was drunk. I stopped the car outside and said, "This is where you keep coming to get help and it doesn't work. You've been over 100 times this year and it just doesn't work." Then I drove to the crematorium and said,

"It's one step from that hospital to here." I quoted James to him, "Resist the devil and he will flee." I took him home and we prayed together. He said, "I'm not strong enough to stop, mate." I told him, "But you don't need to be strong. You need to be weak." I left him. Within the next two weeks he had been admitted into the hospital and died of an alcohol-induced heart attack at fifty years of age.

I felt the man refused to accept the grace God was giving him. He had accepted God, prayed every day, but he wouldn't accept the grace. The journey we had driven became a reality as I drove again to that same crematorium.

To be free we must learn to live free. Yes, we are saved. But are we still held down by the guilt and shame of the past or are we prepared to let the Lord have that as well? I felt that the man was still carrying the guilt and, because he was saved, perhaps the Lord took him to relieve him of the guilt. This man loved the Lord, he was saved. But he still carried the burden, so perhaps the Lord took him to lift the burden.

There was a man in his thirty's, a drug addict, not homeless, but full of pride and ego. He felt self-sufficient. He was good looking and quite healthy in appearance which led him to believe he was not in as bad shape as he was, but the amount of drugs he was using was bound to catch up with him. He was a womanizer. He was likeable, very caring in a lot of ways. When he was well enough, he would do almost anything to help anybody. He got to a point where he had lost a lot of weight due to drug use and he was struggling. He rang me one day and asked if there was anything I could do, if there was any way I could help him.

I went to see him. I told him I could pray for him but that no human power can help addiction, only God could help him. If we could do it on our own, he would already be clean. The man was so resistant to the gospel, even though I shared how my life had changed, how others' lives had changed, he was still unable to believe. He wouldn't accept prayer because he didn't think that would change his life.

He was not eligible for further drug and alcohol treatment as additional treatment funding had been refused because they thought that he was a bad risk. I offered to try to get him in to a free Christian treatment centre, but when I said the word "Christian" he absolutely winced, his shoulders tightened, and he didn't want anything to do with it. A week later he called me again and said, "Can you get me into that place, I can't carry on like this, I can't." I took him to the Christian rehab, and got him in. He lasted two days and left.

He went home and really, really struggled, but over the next six months he did get clean. However, he then became a mocker of faith and of God. He felt he had done what health personnel had said he couldn't do. He believed there was no God and felt that he was the proof of that. As we talked, I would ask him how he was feeling inside? Did he have inner peace? I could tell peace was missing in the man's life. The man just continued with an arrogance that he could get through by himself, he didn't need God.

Unfortunately, in less than six months this young man, who had everything to live for, relapsed and died. This raises the question of why some people can accept the gospel and others can't. All could see that the man had no peace, it was obvious, but he was really deaf and blind to the Word. He was not a bad man, just a prideful one. There are some things for which only the Lord knows the answer.

My own experience has shown it is the power of the Gospel that sets people free, not only from addiction, but also from themselves. Although some are miraculously set free, intense detox is essential for many and that, along with faith, brings a person through to a point where they can accept the power of the Gospel. To accept the Gospel we must participate, we must respond. If God is everything and we own nothing, everything we have in this life is on loan and belongs to God, so we should just look after it. Sometimes we live life like we are never going to die, like it's all in the here and now. We can't see what is right in front of us until sometimes when we see it too late.

There was a day when I was feeling poorly, just didn't feel well, and realized that I had no empathy or compassion for other people. I prayed and asked the Lord to release me from this feeling. It was about six in the morning and I decided to go for a walk to clear my head. I hadn't gone more than twenty steps when a man came up and said, "Can you help me?" There was nobody else around. I said, "Yeah, I can help you."

"I'm hungry," replied the man. There were two things I could have done—give him some money which was in my pocket or give him time and take him to eat with me. My natural instinct was to put my hand in my pocket to give him money, but I felt the Lord saying, "No." I put the man in my car and took him to McDonalds for breakfast.

The man was very, very hungry and was eating very quickly. He was also talking very, very fast. During the conversation it became apparent that he was mentally ill as he was very frightened of life, of the people around him. When we finished eating, he asked me to drop him back in town. As we went outside it started to rain heavily. The man didn't have a coat, so I gave him mine. We got in the car and I was about to drive to drop him off when the man noticed the tattoo of the cross that I have on my left hand. He said, "That's Jesus, isn't it?" I said, "Yes." The man said, "Then I have to pray for you." He prayed with compassion, thanking God that I was compassionate for feeding him and giving him a coat to wear; he prayed protection over me and that I would continue to see what God wanted me to do and do it. When he prayed, he was transformed. He was calm; his voice had changed. His whole demeanor changed. His body was relaxed. He went from a tormented soul to a peaceful calmness and that atmosphere filled the car. When he finished praying, he took hold of my arm and put it on his own shoulder and said, "Mick, pray for me." I prayed for protection over him, for peace in his mind. I thanked God for sending him to teach me. Together we met Christ.

As I was dropping him off, he asked if he could have a copy of the Gospel of John that he had seen in the car. As he was walking away, I got out of the car and the man turned around and smiled and waved. As I waved back, I felt that everything I had prayed for earlier that morning, before I had gotten out of bed, had been answered. I felt full of love, compassion and empathy. I got back in my car and gave a prayer of thanksgiving.

I sat quietly and thought about the Kingdom of God; what it means. I realized that it is most certainly the opposite of what the world is because the person who was hungry, cold, and lonely was the one that brought Christ to me. It wasn't the other way around. To not serve is to not allow God to work in one's life. It's only in serving that one can see and feel God. The people who are struggling the most in the material world seem to be the ones that God chooses to teach the rest of us, and also, to minister to us.

I learned that God speaks to people through the most unlikely people we come across; sometimes through people we might not even like. It raised the question in my mind, "Who do I not listen to because I don't particularly like them?" A short list came immediately to mind. I decided to make a conscious effort to listen to those people. Within the next two to three days I had listened to them all. They each told me something I had never heard before. The things they shared were quite big things. One told me he thought Sarah and I should be attending a church together. I knew this was right, but I didn't want to listen. I had to go against my own will to find the truth. Another was a general conversation asking if you must seek a ministry, find a way to serve in the church, and do you have to have the backing of the pastor to minister? Once again, I didn't want the answers I instantly got from the Holy Spirit. I thought my way was the best because I know myself best. But my eyes were beginning to open and I thought, "Wow! God's still speaking to me today."

I found that the bigger things that needed to be changed or adjusted to move myself forward were coming from the people that I would never have previously listened to because of my own pride and prejudice. As I thanked God for showing me that, I instantly realized that I was no longer judging these people...I was seeing them completely differently.

Again, the Kingdom of God is the opposite of the world. In the world, we don't listen to people because we don't like them and don't want to hear what they have to say. This seems to create a natural prejudice. In the Kingdom of God, we listen, and the prejudice instantly disappears. Sometimes this is easy and other times it is difficult. The personal battle is with self; to let go of self and to trust. It is in trusting in God while listening to other people and not trusting in other people. It's either listening to people or listening to God through people. Colossal difference.

I wanted compassion so I would feel better again. God gave me compassion for those I didn't particularly like—and I began to understand the importance of loving those who are different. The lesson came from God, but it came through a homeless, hungry, cold, mentally ill man, not from a pastor or spiritual leader. It came from suffering love.

I have observed that with people in addiction, abuse, or whatever, when there is a refusal to accept God and His truth they usually physically die without hope. I can think of scores of people to whom I have tried to carry the gospel but for one reason or another they have been either unwilling or unable to accept it. I have started to realize that obedience is about responding to God, not the outcome; the outcome is something completely different—it is not up to me. A separation from self and a closeness to God is the best advice I can give to anyone who is in ministry.

I have seen people literally dragged back from the gates of hell—sometimes quickly and sometimes slowly. I have also seen people listen to the message and reject it and take their own lives; sometimes deliberately, sometimes accidentally through overdose. It seems that the prayer when desperation hits people should be for their willingness to accept faith. People don't realize there is a choice and once one makes that choice the Holy Spirit will help him/her through whatever he/she is facing.

In the people who have been freed, I have seen communities being built by sharing prayer times together and by going out to help others. I have seen faith communities growing stronger and stronger. I have also seen the opposite—a community of sin being brought together and growing stronger and stronger. I see homeless and addicted people coming together, becoming more organized as gangs in the United Kingdom. It's becoming more and more dangerous on the street. When you see a person sitting and begging; you think of them as separate individuals, but most likely they are part of an organized group. It becomes harder to break through with Christ because the power of that community is very, very strong and they are less likely to let someone in to preach the message. They will accept material help but only want what you have to give physically. People must grow on a spiritual basis but it's getting much more difficult to break through to the people who want to remain in this world. Those groups naturally exclude people and the people they exclude are the ones that more easily give themselves to Christ. Even when the others pretend to be interested, they are interested only in material things, not at all interested in hearing about Christ. When they see the cross tattooed on my hand, they will turn their head away, sometimes pushing my hand away.

This growing problem of an out and out hatred for God—being driven by a force of evil doesn't seem to be recognized by those who are going out from the church and is, therefore, not being addressed. People need to understand they are battling the principalities of darkness and there is a spiritual war being waged as well as physical addiction and homelessness. This is organized evil, and it's growing. On one occasion, I had two men approach me. One said, "Why do you come around here with your gentle voice? Your words are not wanted here." It was like a physical threat. When I asked him what was wrong with having a gentle voice, the man replied, "We don't want what you have to offer and we're not going to let you." They didn't clarify what they were not going to let me do. I didn't leave, they left. On another occasion I was talking with a few people. One said, "Can you stop? Your eyes are shining, and I can't stand it. It's making me feel sick." Another walked over and vomited. And the other completely turned away, he couldn't look at me.

Another time I sat down to talk with a man who was obviously mentally and spiritually ill. The man said, "Who sent you?" I replied, "Nobody. I've just come to see how you are and if you need anything." He said, "No, that's a lie, God sent you and there is nothing here for you, Michael." It freaked me out because the man knew my name. I left because the man was agitated but prayed for the man as I walked away. When I turned around to look at him, the man laughed at me and started to hit himself on the head.

Sometimes in these situations I don't know how to listen to God because fear gets in the way. Sometimes I walk away and other times I stand my ground. Trying to do God's will in that moment and in that situation, I don't always know how to respond in a dangerous situation. It's an area I've been praying about. I've had people threated to kill themselves if I prayed for them, even before I told them I was a Christian or offered to pray for them. I've had that happen several times.

To work out the will of God I had to learn how to be still and see in my mind when I pray. I sometimes see two paths;

one is dark and if I walk down that path it rips my feet and I can't see where I'm going. Then there is a gap, and the other path is a shining white, marble-type, smooth path with no obstacles in the way, and that's God's will. In my mind, when I step over and bridge that gap, that's my free will, and it's only then that God speaks to me because I am in God's will. But if I have a foot on each path, I become confused and can't discern. The more time I spend praying to discern the will of God the easier it becomes to know the will of God.

From what I see in the world and as I observe people's actions and reactions, I believe and acknowledge that there is a great spiritual battle going on because I have experienced it. The more I realize that God wants only the best for me, the easier it has been to cross over to the shiny path because I know God's way is best, even in those times when I must go against my own will. I have noticed that when I have gone against myself and gone with God's will, I felt free from self, from the bondage of self, and that is the time when remarkable things happen for me and for others.

It's from that experience that my thinking has been changed. My morals have been transformed; I don't smoke, all the things I wanted to keep for myself are gone, my mind has changed, I don't think like I once thought. At one point every other word was a swear word and now I don't swear. This has all come about through the action of stepping over from my will to God's will. The people I have met who ended up physically dying didn't have the ability or the will to step over from the dark path; they couldn't see, or didn't want to see, that there was another way. What I am seeing in ministry is that there is a spiritual battle that is organized and growing. If there is no willingness, or no prayer for willingness, it is difficult for those turning their backs on the light to change because they don't want to be willing. I am reminded of Jesus asking, "Are you willing?" and the truth is that for many people the answer is, "No, I am not willing." Some people want to keep the sin, but they don't want to accept the consequences. The gospel message is that the consequences of sin is death and it is an important message for all people. Prayer with real confidence against this kind of darkness is the only effective new beginning that I have ever seen. It's important for a believer to be certain when praying, to know that when you pray in the name of Jesus something always happens. One may not see immediate results, but something always happens when one prays with confidence in the name of Jesus. We don't decide the outcome, but we are called to be faithful in prayer. One of the biggest enemies of Christ is fear and the only answer to fear is faith.

Over a period of a few months I had been living a less healthy lifestyle. I was involved in studying, not getting much exercise, making poor diet choices. Life circumstances provided opportunities for me to eat rubbish and ignore my wellbeing. I was aware that since I have an addictive nature, this is something that I could not allow to get out of control, so I was praying about it. I couldn't seem to get an answer. I felt like I was being lazy but also making excuses because I had lots of work to do. I couldn't seem to get a balance on what I knew I should be doing. And I didn't seem to be getting an answer which was frustrating as I always feel like God speaks.

I was driving and praying, "Lord, just give me an answer. What should I do? What do I need to change?" I stopped at the traffic light. There was a car beside me with a middle age man driving. The man pipped his horn and lowered his window. I lowered my window. The man looked straight across at me and said, "You're greedy, you." I was stunned! I felt angry at what the man said! I wanted to give him a smack, thinking, "You don't even know me!" The man continued, "You've got two pair of glasses on your head." And then the other driver laughed. It was true. I had the glasses I wear for dyslexia on my head and my driving glasses on my eyes. The man drove off. I pulled to the side of the road and thanked God for showing me what my sin was in the situation. It was greed. I was eating what I didn't need to eat because it was easier, it was comfortable, but it was unhealthy. It didn't make me feel good; I felt agitated but didn't know why, which is why I had cried out to God. I had not recognized it as greed. For a full week every time I would pick up my Bible the topic would be idolatry and how idolatry became greed. I couldn't escape it.

After a week, even though I knew what the sin was, I had not done anything about it. So, I did what I had done in the past and thanked God for showing me the sin and asked God to give me the strength to do what I needed to do. The minute I accepted the fact that the way I was using food in my lifestyle was sin, I was changed inside. I was able to make the necessary lifestyle changes, went back to the gym, started eating the right foods, and as a result felt so much better. Listening to God means that we must embrace the truth we don't want to hear. God speaks in a way that is crystal clear if we will allow Him to speak to us.

I could have rejected what the man said as it was so random. I could have ignored what the man said, but I recognized this was an answer to what I had just been praying about. I recognized that my immediate—thirty-second response—was sinful. I wanted to be angry and insulted straight away. I was gobsmacked[15], offended, and then grateful all within a few minutes. I feel that's a cycle that happens when we are confronted with our sin, we don't want to recognize it for what it is, but if we accept the truth and ask for forgiveness, we can have not only the forgiveness but also the peace that goes with it.

Once I accepted God's truth, I was easily able to make the lifestyle changes and began feeling so much better. Because I was able to become aware of the big sin that was once in my life and ask for forgiveness that transformed my life, it now seems easier for me to recognize the little sins. Untreated greed would eventually lead me back to the bigger sin which would make me more and more susceptible to a life of addiction. Confession of that sin and allowing God to

---

[15] Utterly astounded, astonished

cleanse me and change my lifestyle prevented that from happening.

When sin takes full hold, we become blind; we can't see and acknowledge our own sin. We tend to blame circumstances, other people, anything but the sin that is within us. When the Lord shines His light on us it is easier to take responsibility and He will take us through the change. We respond in obedience to the grace God has given us.

After the incident I was grateful to know that God is with me. When I get off the right path, God finds a way to put me back on track, but obedience is crucial for that to happen. The more I read my Bible, the more I see God in the world around me. If I miss reading my Bible for more than a few days—which now rarely happens—there is a type of disconnection. So, I have learned the importance of staying in the Word in order to stay on track.

Once after a time of sharing with a friend where we were both overwhelmed by the power of God's amazing grace, I felt almost a regeneration of spirit, a spiritual humility that was beyond a conscious feeling; something bigger than my own awareness; a totally different feeling. I felt as though I was not breathing air but breathing love. Over the course of the day it got stronger and stronger and by evening that sense of love was overwhelming.

By the time the weekend came I was feeling a deep peace and found myself with two hours to spare on a Saturday evening. I went through a McDonalds drive-through and as I was ordering food, I strongly felt like I was to order double, so I did—I ordered two sandwiches and two coffees. I then drove to a little spot where I regularly go to eat and pray. I was still conscious of the experience that we had shared during the week. As I was praying, I heard the same voice that told me to order double tell me to go to the supermarket. It was nighttime, and I knew there wouldn't be anybody there. I had eaten my sandwich but still had my coffee. I drove to the nearest supermarket and heard the voice again, saying, no not that one. I kept driving and ended up a few miles away, at the very supermarket my friend and I had discussed the previous week.

Someone had given me £20 to use for ministry and that was in my coat pocket. I parked, not expecting to see anyone there. I was surprised to find a man sitting on a blanket which was unusual for that time of day. I prayed again, and the same voice said, "That's the one." I opened my car boot where I had a pair of new, warm socks and I put them in my pocket and took the coffee and sandwich and walked over to the man.

I asked the man if it was okay if I sat down next to him and the man said yes. I said, "You look very cold." He showed me his hands which were bright purple and swollen, which was partly from drug use, but it was absolutely freezing, and the man was so cold! I gave him the coffee and the sandwich and then I remembered the socks. I took them out of my pocket and put them over the man's hands, using them as gloves. The man turned to me and looked me right in the eye and said, "He's sent you, hasn't He?" My first thought was that he was quite mentally ill, but I reassured him and said, "Yeah, He has sent me." I wanted to believe the man was referring to God, but I really thought it was just the illness. His next words almost melted me, He said, "Thank you, Michael." I had never met him before. I asked the man how he knew my name and the man replied, "You are the angel Michael." I didn't know whether to feel good or bad because he thought I was an angel! But I felt that God had sent me, and I was supposed to be there. I asked him if he wanted to sit in the car where it was warmer, and he said, "No, I've got to get the money together." I knew he would stay out all night if he needed to.

Then I heard the voice again, "Give him your coat." "Oh, no!" I thought. I really liked that coat and thought maybe I should go buy him a blanket or something.   Then I remembered, I had been given that coat two years ago and realized I had received it to give at this time. I took the blanket off the man and put the coat on him and then put the blanket around him. The man thanked me and then put his arms around me. I felt him clinging to me; the man didn't want to let go. He said that two days before he had been sleeping in a sleeping bag under a subway where it was dry, and someone walked by and kicked him so hard that it split the back of his head open. He said he wanted to kill himself after that, but God had told him that Michael would come and help him. And I guess he did, just not the winged one!

As I was leaving, I realized I had left the £20 in the pocket of the coat and thought that was the best way to give. God had given it; I didn't even know I had done so. I turned around and went back to the man and told him there was some money in the jacket, hoping that the man would go to a warmer place. That's all I wanted for the man. The man reached in the pocket and pulled out the £20 note. He cried and said, "Thank you, Michael." Even though I know I am no angel, at that moment I felt I was his angel because the man believed it and his prayer was answered.

As I drove away, I thought about how God works. How one person sees something one way and another person saw something differently, but God brought us together for His purpose. The man felt he had been entertaining an angel— but so did I, the man was my angel.

Everything I had given had been given to me to use but nothing was used in the way that I would have given it—the socks were used for gloves, the money was given through forgetfulness, the coat was given not in a way I intended. I would have found the person then bought the coffee—not the other way around. It was all upside down by human standards but all in God's plan.

One day I went to see an old friend who is not a Christian. He's a man with a good heart, but definitely not a Christian. As I went up to my friend's door the woman next door asked for a cigarette. I don't smoke but got a cigarette from my friend, who didn't want to give it to her. My friend said he was tired of her mooching, she smokes crack. The man had bitterness toward her; the resentment he felt toward her was evident as he was talking. As the conversation went forward, he said the woman had a little girl and the little girl was always scrounging for food and he didn't want anything to do with either of them. He thought they were just scroungers and he didn't want them near him.

I asked if he was saying the little girl was always hungry. The man said, "They've got no food—she's spent it all on drugs—they've got no food." But he showed no emotion. I asked him for £10. The man said, "No way! You're one of those mental Christians! If I give you a tenner [16] you will go and buy them food." I said, "You're right. You give me a tenner and I will go and buy them food." The man refused. I got up and said, "I'm going to go get something and I'll be back." The man just shook his head and as I left said, "You're just helping her to smoke crack; you're not doing either of them any good."

I went to the market and bought about £20 of food that fit in two bags. As I went around, I seemed to be putting things randomly in the basket. As I started toward the check-out I thought, "I'll go back and get some cheese." Then I thought, "What's wrong with me? Why am I going back for cheese?" But I went and picked up the cheese. As I walked away, I thought, "That's not the right cheese!" So, I went back and

---

[16] Ten pounds or a ten-pound note

swapped the cheese. As I was walking away, I thought maybe my friend was right, maybe I was nuts!

I drove back and pulled up to the house to find the little girl out in her garden. I went over to the fence and gave the little girl the two bags and told her to give them to her mummy. I went in my friend's house and resumed drinking coffee as my friend sat shaking his head.

A knock came on the door. It was the mother and child. The mum said, "Thank you." The little girl handed me a picture of an angel with two shopping bags. In the childish drawing I could see the wings of the angel and the two bags the angel was carrying. On the back was a shopping list. Everything I had bought was on the list—even the cheese— the right kind of cheese! The mum said, "How did you know? We wrote this last night. I have no money, but we wrote the list thinking when we got money, we would go buy these things. How did you know?" I said, "I didn't, but Jesus knew." The little girl said, "The angel forgot the chocolate biscuits." And right on the bottom of the list was chocolate biscuits. I remembered that someone had given me a box of chocolate biscuits for Christmas and they were in the boot of the car. I invited them outside. They all came outside to watch as I opened the boot, pulled out the biscuits and gave them to the little girl. The mother broke down in tears. She put her arms around me as we were walking back into the house. The little girl had such a beautiful smile.

I sat down with my friend who asked, "What's that all about? How did that happen?" I said, "It's that mental Christianity you talked about."

My friend said, "I won't be but a minute." He got up and took a pack of cigarettes and gave them to the lady next door. He came back in and said he had told her he has his tea[17] every day at 5:00 and if the little girl knocked on his door between 4:30 and 4:45 she could eat with him or she could take the food home. He would feed her every day as long as he lived there.

As he sat down telling me this, I said, "I thought they were scum. I thought she was just a scrounging drug addict. I thought you would never give them anything." The man replied, "I was wrong. God forgive me." I prayed, and the man closed his eyes. The man didn't respond but he held his hands together. He had seen God at work. Jesus fed that little girl not just for one meal but for many, by building a relationship between neighbours.

The lesson is we really do need to love our neighbours. What should the Christian response be? How do we show love to other people? Jesus wasn't in the cheese and in the biscuits, but He was definitely in the giving!

This event may not stop the woman from using crack. But it might make her stop and ask questions. Why did this happen? Was God in it? There was a child that was hungry. I had a choice. It was how I acted. We don't need to punish people for their sins; that's up to God. We have enough sins of our own.

---

[17] Tea – widely used as a name for the evening meal, especially in the North of England

In that one hour my friend saw the world in a different light. He saw there was an alternative. The question is, "Who benefitted?" The answer is everyone! Each person involved benefitted from the experience.

I was talking with a Christian friend who had recently ended a serious relationship. As we talked, I tried to console him, just listening to him through the pain. I noticed this huge desire in my friend to compete with his ex-girlfriend, and doubly with me. I noticed this competition in his emotions, blaming her, complaining about what she was doing to him, it all had a competitive edge. It divided; there was no chance of peace or reconciliation. My friend had been receiving other advice, which was also divisive, telling him what he needed to do. It divided, made a competition of the former relationship. As I was talking with my friend, I realized I was doing exactly the same thing; I was trying to take ownership of the situation and give advice on that basis, which too was creating competition which separated. I stopped myself.

I thought about how competitive human beings are, even in conversation. I realized in everything that competes there is a winner and a loser. But when you stop competing that's when some sort of restoration can take place, some sort of coming back together, some sort of freedom. It's realizing that you are no longer racing against somebody else, the race is over, and healing can begin from that point.

117

I gave my friend advice based more on my understanding of the cross which to me is the powerlessness that Christ showed as He went to the cross. He laid down all his power and became powerless, deliberately. I realized that if we as human beings translate this powerlessness of the cross to every area of our life, even our conversation, then the power of God can be in everything we do.

I gave my friend advice based not on myself, not trying to take ownership of his situation, not trying to take sides, not trying to split the situation into two camps. I found the results were very different as my friend started to realize that he had no real control over the situation. He started to lay his power and his bitterness to one side, and he became powerless himself. His anger turned to tears and healing began. There were no longer two sides.

This experience got me thinking about the foolishness of the cross and how everything in the world seems to be about exerting your own power to fix things—whether it be trying to quit smoking, trying to get a job, or your studies.

I started to pray, and it came to mind that the entire systems of the world are set up to compete. I feel we even compete in conversations with one another. We compete emotionally to get our own emotional needs met. Every mortal thing I could think about or see was a competition.

I went back and read 1 Corinthians 1 and 2 again and started to wonder what Paul meant about this foolishness. What should this foolishness look like? As I read on, I found that Paul was the example of the gospel--he continually, deliberately made himself powerless in every situation. For example, he didn't need to work as a tentmaker, but he laid the power of his education to one side to announce the gospel. He allowed himself to be beaten for the sake of the gospel. He made himself powerless, he didn't compete. He surrendered himself powerless. When there is no power there is no competition. When human beings stop competing it seems the gospel message can be heard, seen, and lived out. By its very nature competition divides. Powerlessness unites.

I regularly meet with a friend who is new in faith. We talk about the Bible. In these meetings there is no competition, no teacher, and no pupil. We both seem to learn from each other. It's like we leave our power at the door. When we pray together the power that enters the room is like nothing either of us have ever experienced before. This happens every single time we pray on this basis. It's like the atmosphere in the room changes and we can both sense a background noise, a white noise, the pitch is a different sound and we can both hear it. We are both always overwhelmed with the need for prayer and when we finish praying we each notice that the other looks slightly different— our features are slightly different just for a short time—and this peaceful feeling rests, not just on us but in the atmosphere—it's in the room—it's bigger than the two of us. That atmosphere and feeling stays and disappears very, very slowly and even when I leave it is like the atmosphere goes with me. As I get in my car to drive away the atmosphere goes with me. I am learning that as a Christian I need to leave my strength and my power to one side so that God can work through me instead of me trying to work through God.

It seems so simple but, yet the urge is in me to constantly want to compete. To compete even in conversation, in thinking, in studying, in everything. I am finding that to connect with God on a deeper level I must intentionally ask God to help me put myself to one side so that I can see where I am dividing myself and others. This seems true for most people I meet on a daily basis so I feel there is division in the body of Christ—where Christ asks for unity. Paul's gospel of powerlessness is more relevant now than ever before.

My experience has been that to be in God's presence and to be in His Word I have to constantly go inward—be still and feel my love for Jesus. When my mind starts to get distracted, I say a few words of praise and that takes me back where I can be still and spend time in the presence of God. It is silent prayer; worshipping God without self. I find that these are the times God tends to show Himself more to me. The feeling of God's presence overwhelms and then things begin to happen outside. It's never the other way around.

Once when I was being still, being in the presence of God, as there was a situation for which I didn't know how to pray, I decided to be quiet for unspoken prayer. I had asked the Lord what to pray for. Within a few minutes of being still I was interrupted by a text message from a friend that asked me to lift him up in prayer for his health was getting worse; that he was in a fight for his life and needed prayer. I prayed that the Lord would lift him up—not only physically but in his spirit. I also asked another friend to pray for him. I met the man who had texted me about four days later and he said, "I want to tell you something. It sounds really stupid." He was praying, and he felt that God literally lifted him out of his body; that he had never experienced anything like that before. In that moment, his own pride was pointed out to him and the Lord told him he was forgiven for that. The man understood that the Lord knew he had suffered because of people who had sinned against him. However, the Lord had forgiven those people—and so must he.

The power of prayer is sharing with other human beings—it is not just about yourself—it's the humility of sharing your weakness with another person that gives strength to the prayer. It's not "me" and God—it's "we" and God. There are ways to share of yourself in prayer with others.

Sometimes when we don't know what to pray for, or when we feel proud, confused, and defective in some way, we need to go further in—to experience this beautiful, wonderful silent prayer. This beautiful silent prayer brings results.

The more I practice this kind of prayer, the more I feel God changing me inwardly and outwardly. There have been times when I have been able to physically see things I have never seen before. Sometimes I feel as though I can almost see into someone's soul; almost like I could reach in and pull a black thing out. It's a wonderful feeling. It is like the Lord is blowing the dark from the other person. It is like I can physically see the dark in the other person and pull it out to the Lord. It seems when we go deeper into the Lord and lose ourselves, we can see deeper into other people and know how God wants to minister to them through us. When we see them through God's eyes, we can cut out all the rubbish and see what they really need.

This kind of prayer has become more prominent in my life which is allowing me to go deeper and to participate with God. It is a humbling experience but deeply experiencing God's love allows Him to do the changing—I don't have to try to do it on my own. All we have to do is just stop! Be still! Experience God! We don't need to try to figure out who or what God is—we just need to experience God. This is the way I determine God's will for my life, and I believe it is the same for everyone. The real will of God is that we love Him. All other things will come from that. When we practice being still and keep at it until we can be completely still, it's like walking with God in the garden—it's what we were created to be and to do—to be in His presence. I really do believe, as it says in Luke, that the Kingdom of God is within you—within each one of us. We go inward first so that we can go outward. Going inward is to love God with all your heart, mind and soul so that you **can** go outward and love your neighbour as yourself.

A friend gave me a lovely warm coat with a hood, and I put it in the boot of the car. The next day I went into the village for breakfast early in the morning. I saw a man begging but the man looked like he was warm, he had a furry hood up and was wrapped in a sleeping bag. I didn't feel like the man needed the coat. I just kind of watched him out of the corner of my eye. As I was walking to my car the Lord said, "Give him the coat." "But he doesn't need the coat, he's got one!" I protested. The response was clear, "Give him the coat." I got the coat out of my boot. Even though I still didn't think the man needed the coat, I also took a pair of new wool socks from the boot. I put the socks in the coat pocket and walked over to the man and said, "Do you need this?" The man's eyes filled with tears, he stood up. He didn't have a coat—he only had a hood. He was so grateful! He had shoes on but no socks. In all the times that I have helped people I don't know when I have ever seen someone as grateful. I had decided he didn't need anything, but the Lord knew exactly what he needed. I didn't say much to the man other than, "The Lord bless you." To which the man replied, "He already has." God gives everything freely. We can't decide what to give—we must leave that to God. That's so, so important. We must let God decide what we give and not determine in our own minds what we should give. It makes such a difference for all concerned.

I am learning to give on the basis of obedience rather than from myself. When we give there is an exchange involved whether we know it or not. We want them to be happy with what we give, we want them to be grateful. But rather than being concerned about their response, we just need to listen to God. It's a completely different kind of giving, more holy, and one never knows to whom he/she is giving. Our eyes don't always see the truth. We need God to open our eyes so we can see under the sleeping bag, so we can see there is no coat. I thought I was giving a coat to someone who didn't need a coat, but God knew the need.

Don't be in competition with God. Surrender to Him when He speaks, and things will get to where they are supposed to be. It's so humbling to realize we know nothing. Not even how to give. To have the knowledge of God's will and the power to carry it out we really need to listen—and obey. Sometimes what we think we see is not necessarily the reality. Sometimes it's not just the physically poor who have great need and we can overlook those who are well dressed and smiling but are dying and hurting on the inside. We need to be sensitive to how God speaks to us about those people as well.

I am probably the poorest that I've ever been in my life, but I don't feel poor, I feel wealthy. There's a certainty that whatever I need, I will receive. It's a strange feeling that I have not previously experienced. My security is no longer in money or things and this is not something I chose to happen. It is something that God brought into my life.

In my earlier years as a Christian, I had a car but no money for petrol. I was too proud to ask for money and didn't know what I was going to do. As I prayed, I felt that since I didn't have the money to go anywhere, I was where God wanted me to be. As it turned out there was a person who came to campus who was not in a good place and I was able to connect with him and help him over the weekend. When Monday came, money for petrol was given to me. I learned that if I don't have money to go, then I need to accept that I am where God wants to use me.

Someone recently asked me how I know I am doing God's will. How do you know it is God? The best answer I could give is, "When it's not about me. That's when wonderful, miraculous things happen." When I feel an urge— a prompting--and act on it, it's never once been about me. It's a prompting to serve and it may even cost—physically, emotionally, or financially. But it's in those moments when one responds that the miracles happen. In the times you get it wrong, you are still doing good deeds and God appreciates you serving. In fact, you can't even be sure you got it wrong, because you don't always see the final consequences.

The love that comes from giving is unbelievable. The power of God is amazing. It's not about doing without. It's about trusting and giving what you are asked to give. To obey God as soon as you can. Obeying God means that I don't mask things when I've made a mistake. It means going to someone and saying, "I was really wrong. Will you forgive me?" To ask someone to forgive your faults is giving—it's not just physical obedience, it's also spiritual obedience. It may be someone we don't even particularly like but knowing that he/she is the right person to go to and going, that's obedience to God. Obedience to God is the Gospel—Jesus' obedience even to death. Maybe obedience requires us to be much humbler than we want to be as human beings. I sometimes notice that Christians are quite readily obedient to themselves and to one another, but not necessarily obedient to God.

To be obedient is to show your flaws as well as your assets for when you hide your flaws you are less authentic. This is not deliberate; it is the way of the world. But there is value in being authentic, in showing what and who we are. Obedience to God is a journey, sometimes we learn it through pain and suffering, sometimes through joy, but it is the highway to holiness. Through the listening, waiting, not deciding for yourself, that's when He picks you up. When you decide to stop trying to fight your own battles and submit your will to His will. That's when you find peace.

I met a man who was a gangster, collecting drug debts, a huge man in stature and size, scary almost. He was heavy into drugs and alcohol. I was able to help him along the journey of becoming free from drugs and alcohol. On that journey the man became a Christian.

I explained to him that he needed to turn his troubles over to God. I told him he could give everything over to God, everything he had ever done. I explained how he could pray and ask God for this. The man wanted to do this and as he prayed the power of the Holy Spirit fell upon him, he had never experienced that kind of love in his entire life. His thinking and actions have been transformed since that day.

A lot of his problems resulted from information regarding his adoption. He learned he had brothers. He found and met his birth mother and father while he was still on drugs and it wasn't a positive experience. After his conversion he re-connected with them on a different basis. He started to learn about his mother, what she had been through; circumstances that had happened to her; why he had been put up for adoption. He began to have compassion rather than anger toward her. He felt identification with his birth father who was also an aggressive man who suffered from addiction. The man was now able to feel compassion rather than anger toward his father.

He went to visit his father, who lives separately from his mother. His father was very ill. He was praying that his father could find Jesus as he recognized that was what was missing in his father's life. He sat by his father's bed and prayed silently, and when he left, he had peace and felt that his father had peace as well.

A few days later the man rang and said he had just received a call to go see his father as he was nearing death. As he entered the room his father had his eyes closed. The man took hold of his father's hand and asked if he knew who he was, and his father squeezed his hand. The man has been struggling with eternal life; what does that mean? How does it impact life now? As the man prayed for his father while holding his hand, he felt love pouring through him and he received understanding of what eternal life through Christ meant.

He called again that evening and said, "This is a real miracle, mate. I could never have gotten through an experience like this without drugs or taking a drink. It would have been impossible. It's a real miracle! And the biggest miracle is I don't even want one." He said it was a message to his biological family, how to forgive and how to love –the meaning of suffering love. He said, "All the things you told me have shown themselves to be true in this one circumstance and I now understand what you mean when you say the truth will set you free. I now know what that means."

He is mesmerized by how he can feel these emotions but still feel peace. In real-life situations that were full of despair, he was still filled with hope. He was still expecting his father to pass away, but he waited with no fear. He waited in hope and love. He knew that he would be able to support his mother and his brothers through the death. Instead of feeling like the outsider he felt like the one in the middle pulling everybody together. And all he had actually done was turn up. He determined where the fear was; the fear became hope; the hope became love; and the love became peace.

To see this wild giant of a man who could snap somebody with his bare hands, who had verbally testified that he hated God--if there was a God he hated him--to see him through the power of Christ pouring out love in a painful situation and thanking Christ for what He has done and what He is doing, brings an immense sense of gratitude.

The man took me into his life because I took him into mine and we get to share the love of brotherhood because of a shared love of Christ. Faith is well and good when life is good. But when life is tough, and you only have faith, that's when it is the most powerful. Not only are you transformed but so are the people around you. Just a few months before this man couldn't hold relationships together, he could not hold himself together, but through Christ he found a cornerstone. As I watched the man build his life on the cornerstone of Christ it strengthens my faith as well.

This was the type of man of whom everyone was afraid. He looked dangerous and he looked angry. People wouldn't even look him in the eye. No one had explained the gospel to him because they were afraid of him. I didn't find him—the man found me in a random, mistaken phone call one Saturday morning. This led to a friendship and a witness to Christ so that we share an equal seat at the table. Real faith comes from sharing ourselves with one another equally at the table of God. That's where we are transformed.

One of the lessons I learned from this friend was equality in Christ. While I was leading him to faith, he declared he felt that we were the same. He had never felt that before. He either felt beneath people or wanted to be over them, but he felt we were equal. I told him we were. We were both sinners, saved by the grace of God. Gaining understanding from another person of what it feels like to be treated equally in their suffering has had a big impact on me. I've learned that to teach from a place of humility in spirit is much more powerful than teaching from knowledge. Humility in spirit is more beneficial in the transformation process.

A few days later the man called at 3:00 a.m. and was very excited. He drives a grit wagon[18] for salting the roads. He was in the yard loading up and it was raining, wet, and cold. He heard a large cracking sound and thought something had happened to the truck. He got out of the truck and climbed the ladder to look into the bed of the truck. On the top of the truck was a small red book, which turned out to be the New Testament and Psalms. It was 3:00 a.m., in the rain, and the book was completely dry. He picked up the book and went back to the cab of the truck; he was in complete shock; he couldn't believe what was happening.

He called to say, "It's dry, completely dry and there was no one around!" He felt it was a miracle for him. He opened it and beginning to read and found peace. But he said there

---

[18] A sander, salt spreader or salt truck

were some pages ripped out. I asked him to tell me what was before and after—it was the Beatitudes that had been ripped out of the book. Basically, the whole of the Sermon on the Mount. He asked what he should do. I told him that when he went home, he should read the part that was missing and see what he thought. When he did, he was blown away, he said it's everything you have told me, and he realized that his recovery was fully from Christ.

This man who just a few months ago was angry, violent and desperate, now has peace running through the core of his being. He is a transformed human being, unrecognizable from who he was and growing in faith every day.

One afternoon I went to pick up Sarah for a coffee. She was waiting outside when I got there, and she was very glad to see me. She pointed out a man who had made her very uneasy. He offered to sell her some perfume and he was very edgy. She got in the car and I could see the man. I sat there for a minute and could tell the man had a knife up his sleeve. Then I saw the man edging toward a parked taxi and I knew what he had in mind. I told Sarah to stay in the car that I was just going to go help the man a minute.

As I approached the man, I put my arm around him on the side of the knife and told him I had come to help him. The man looked at me, not understanding. I said gently, "I know you have a knife and that you are planning to rob the taxi. I want to help you. If you pull that knife in public you will go to jail for five years, if you put it to his throat you will get seven years, and if you kill him you will spend your life in jail. I want to help you. Someone gave me some money and I want to give you some of that money." "Why would you do that?" the man asked. "Because I love you," I replied. "And Jesus sent me to help you." "I don't believe in that Jesus stuff," the man said. I told him, "That doesn't matter; He still loves you and sent me to give you £10 so you won't go to jail tonight. Jesus sent me so you don't have to go to prison, and nobody gets hurt." The man was stunned. He realized it wasn't about the money, that something bigger was happening, and he said, "How did you know?" I replied, "Jesus told me."

I explained—it wasn't me; Jesus just put me there at the right time. The fact that Jesus had sent me to help him, to keep him out of jail, and to give him some money threw the man into confusion. He just looked at me and said, "What do I do now? I don't know what to do!" I said, "I'll give you the money, I want to buy the knife off of you." I was making it clear that the man was giving me something bad, but that in exchange he would be given something good. I wanted him to understand that Jesus would take the bad and give him something good in return—if the man was willing to do that. We exchanged the knife from his sleeve to mine and I gave him the money. He asked again, "What do I do now?" I knew he was really asking, what do I do with my life now? How do I go on? I told him to pray and thank God; to ask God what He wanted him to do, as God had just given him another chance. The man asked my name and I told him and then I asked the man for his name and he told me. The man put his arms around me and I put my arms around him. He started to cry. I asked if he would pray for me that night and he said he would. I told him I would pray for him as well. And we left...we separated like brothers.

There were four people involved in this incident but only the man and I knew what was happening. No one else was looking on, no one else got involved; it was as though the two of us were in a bubble in time. We alone knew what was happening. I returned to the car within fifteen minutes and Sarah asked if he was okay. I said, "Yes, he's okay and he's going to pray for me tonight. He's all right." I didn't tell her about the knife.

I dropped Sarah back home, went and disposed of the knife as quickly as possible, without making an issue of it. I realized that knives can have a power to them, that a person can feel an attachment to them. Because of my past, I understand that when people are in the dark, they can be attracted to knives, become attached to them, feeling safe with them, putting their trust in the knife rather than something holy.

I do not advocate that everyone should chase after someone who has a knife and is planning to use it. I went because the Holy Spirit directed me to go to the man and it was as though I could see what was going to happen. Because of my past, I understood the man but it was the Holy Spirit who directed the encounter. The Holy Spirit shows me when to intervene and when not to. My part is to act in obedience and under the power of the Holy Spirit rather than on my own inclination.

God uses everything about our character to complete His work. If another person were involved God might have worked entirely different. God has created each of us in different ways and we should allow God to direct us in all our encounters with other people. If we are willing, God will show us how and if/when we are to be involved. Whatever we do should be done in love.

I knew I wasn't taking the knife from the man; it was God taking the knife from the devil. It was the power of God over the power of evil. It was not the knife and not the £10--it was what they represented. Evil was disarmed in the transaction.

I don't go out searching for people, but I've found when I go out in obedience, God brings the people and the resources just in the course of daily life. It's not going out with the idea of being fully equipped; knowing how you are going to serve—but living your life and letting God establish the priorities. Sometimes the priority might be to finish an essay that is due and there will be no unusual encounters in your life. We cannot manufacture when God will use us; we just need to be available when He sends.

I do pray for opportunities and ways to serve. That service might be just to take Dad shopping or to put my arm around my son to encourage him. These, too, are ways God is using me in ministry. My ministry is my life. My life is my ministry. My ministry is not to any particular segment of the population, and not to what people say I should do, but to be obedient when and where God shows me a need.

One morning I went into an Asian grocery shop. A Muslim clerk noticed the tattoo of a cross on my hand and asked if I was a Christian. I said I was. The clerk asked if I thought Jesus was the Son of God and I said yes. The clerk said, "He's a good prophet but he's not God." I said, "He's my God, and you're my brother." I extended my hand and we shook hands and I left the shop.

That night I prayed and asked God what it meant when someone challenges my faith, what should I say? I'm from a predominately Muslim area and probably will be living in that area. My prayer was for understanding.

The following evening Sarah and I were going to a different store in a different town and a man was begging outside the store. The man was homeless and was absolutely freezing. He was so cold! I took off my coat and put it on the man. Sarah went into the store and got some food for him and we gave the man some money. As we turned to walk away the man saw the cross on my hand.

Sarah looked back and said, "He's crying. Why is he crying?" I turned around and went back. I asked the man why he was crying. There was a mosque across the road from where he was sitting. The man said four or five guys had come out of the mosque and came over to talk to him. They told him that if he converted to Islam, he would have a better life: he would have food, somewhere to live, a wife, and money. "But you've just given me the coat off your back and it's still warm," he said.   I said, "That's because it's better to feel peace and love inside than to have anything else, like cars, and a wife. Jesus is really, really with you. Can you feel him?" The man said, "Yes, I can feel Him because I am warm in this coat." And we parted as brothers.

The next day was Sunday.   I got a phone call from the church where I was living and where there was an extra bedroom in my flat. They asked how I felt about someone else moving in. They said he's a nice guy, he's a gambling addict, and he's an Asian Muslim. I said I couldn't wait to meet him!

When we met, we shook hands and sat down together I asked him to tell him me about himself. The man told all about his life and how the gambling had gotten hold of his life. I asked him if he believed in God, did he go to the mosque? He said he didn't go to the mosque, but he thought he did believe in God as he had prayed the week before a place to live. And within the week he had a place to live, and he thought it was God.

I asked him what he thought addiction was and how he could get out of it. The man replied that he had to be very strong with his will power and he could do it. I said, "What if I tell you no matter how strong your will power is it will never work; you will never be able to break your addiction by using your will power."   The man looked stunned and shocked; even fearful. He asked then what was he to do? I asked if I could pray for him. The man agreed. I said, "I'm a Christian, can I pray for you in the name of Jesus?" The man said yes. I first asked if he was sorry for everything he had done to his family, his friends, and to himself. Was he truly, truly sorry? He said he was truly sorry, but he felt so guilty about it. I started to pray, put my hand on the man's shoulder and asked God to forgive his sins, to heal him, and to pour so much love into him that he would know who Jesus was. At that moment my Muslim friend broke down, fell on his knees, and asked Jesus to help him. The man held on to me and just poured out his tears.

All of this came from one conversation about a tattooed cross on my hand and my asking God how to respond; how to act in humility.

I don't know where my new friend will go from here but do know that he has good support. It may not be easy, but he will not be alone.

God told me that it's the love in the giving, taking the coat off and putting it on the beggar while it was still warm that made such a difference. When you ask God when you don't know what to do, or ask Him to show you what something means, God always responds. All you have to do is ask.

I have observed two types of Christians and am still trying to work out the whys and wherefores of these different types of Christians. The first type is the one who missed an appointment because he overslept and will say something like, "If God wanted me there, He would have woken me." The second type is the one that says, "I have missed the appointment, God forgive me for my laziness and help me." Perhaps we are all a mixture of both. The humility that God asks of us is to be truthful in what and who we really are. The more honest we can become about our own sin, the more grateful we are to God when we confess it to Him and experience His forgiveness.

Denial is not just denial of our own circumstances but is denial of our own sin. Can we choose to be humble? Is it a choice? Do we choose to humbly walk with God? Or do we ignore that voice deep within us and hold on to the false humility? There's a wonderful saying: I was once given a badge for being humble, but they took it off me for wearing it. Real humility is to put ourselves to one side. Look at people with spiritual eyes and not worldly eyes; to see what God sees. Do we see a pretty face, or do we see an angry, vulnerable, deceitful person? Do we see with our eyes or do we see with our heart? What is it we actually see?

I knew a man who was in recovery and he was so hard to like. There was a real arrogance about him. He swore a lot. I just disliked the man; everything he stood for and everything he did. I had only to think about him and it would set my teeth on edge. The man had done nothing to me; I just didn't like him. I was taking another person to a recovery meeting and the irritating man asked if he could come along. I was nodding my head yes but that was not the answer in my heart! I was to pick them both up the next night, but the first man cancelled.

I found myself sitting in the car for a drive that would take more than an hour, driving with this man toward whom I had all this unexplainable resentment. As we were driving, the man was telling about himself-- how good he was, how much money he had, and how great he was at the gym. This went on for the first twenty minutes and I said nothing. Finally, I pulled off the road and stopped the car and told the man I wouldn't be but a minute.

I got out of the car, took two big deep breaths and prayed, "Lord forgive me. I'm really struggling with this man. Help me."

I got back in the car and the other man asked, "What's the matter?" I very calmly said, "You've been talking for twenty minutes and all you have done is tell me how good you are, what a great guy you are, and I don't believe you." He asked what I meant. I answered, "I think you are scared. I think you are pretending to be something and somebody you are not. I am really, really sorry that I have not liked you. I find myself getting irritated with you and I am sorry."

The man hung his head and began to sob. I asked him why he was crying. He said he had been abused as a child. He had been put in a children's home. He lifted his shirt and his back was covered with scars from being burned with cigarettes when he was a young child. He had been raped daily and systematically. He couldn't tell people. He couldn't be himself because he didn't know who he was. He had used drugs all his life to escape the mental illness and the pain that went along with being abandoned and abused. He said that no one could ever love him. I pulled the man's face to look at me and told him to look at me. As he looked, he saw my tears. I told him, "There's One that loves us both." I shared a little about my own past and in broad daylight, in the middle of the city, two six foot plus, 17 stone[19] men, covered in tattoos, hugged each other in tears. The man who I had truly despised in my heart became my brother.

We are now friends, sharing the journey together. The man has become a Christian and a new creation. He often reminds me, "Do you remember when you hated me?" God saw the love that I couldn't see. When I got out of the car and asked God to help me, He most certainly did! And that's how you love your enemies—by allowing God to make them your brother or sister.

Until he confessed to me, the man had felt all alone. I knew his boasting was false and I judged him based on what I could see; I did not see him as God sees him. Today the man has become a Christian and is a changed man. He still has a daily struggle fighting the demons, but today he fights them with God's help. He knows he is not alone.

We think we have had a tough life—until we learn what others have experienced. Although he was severely abused, the fact that he is sane and functioning is a credit to God. He doesn't tell everyone what's happened to him but neither does he falsely brag about himself. Now that he can be himself, people are happy to be around him. He no longer

---

[19] A stone is a unit of weight equal to 14 pounds. 17 stones would equal 238 pounds

has to pretend. He's no longer lonely. He's no longer repeatedly abandoned.

I was interviewed for a story to be used in NTC's Link Magazine. I was okay with what was written but had not known I was to be the cover story. I didn't know my picture would be on the front cover and that my story was the student focal point. The cover featured a file photo from two years before taken while I was in class, and a second photo from my student ID card. I was a bit embarrassed to walk around campus and see my picture in the magazine racks.

After the magazine came out, I was sitting in the café and a lady came up and spoke to me privately. She said she had read the article and that it really touched her. I thanked her and asked her why it touched her. She said it was when I said I advised people recovering from addictions to pray differently—to thank God for their suffering because it means that God's changing them. She had never thought that way before. She asked how long I had been free from addiction and I replied for eight years. She started to get teary. I asked if she was okay. She said, "You've filled me full of hope because my brother is a heroin addict and he's been trying for years to get clean. When I read your article, it said you don't pray for people to get clean anymore—you pray for them to find God." She cried and said, "I've been asking

God, selfishly, to get him clean, and now I am going to ask that he finds God."

I told her one of the incidents where I had gotten there just in time to prevent a man from committing suicide. I shared that the man is now doing well. God transformed him.

Two days later she stopped me again and said she has a lady friend who was just coming off heroin and is a Christian. She shared what I had told her with this lady and the two women had broken down in tears and held each other. The other lady asked if it would be all right to pray for people you don't know. Is that allowed? They prayed for the man that had been saved from suicide; that he wouldn't go back to a life of discouragement.

I then realized that although I felt a little bit embarrassed, uncomfortable, because I felt the pictures were pointing to me—God was using what was causing me discomfort to touch others. To see the profound impact the article was having on other people allowed me to thank God for using it in that way.

Perhaps there are times when the Lord will embarrass you and that may be that's a sign that you are giving in to God's will. Now I have God's peace about being on the cover of the magazine. I don't want to be the centre of attention but am realizing it's not about me but rather about giving God glory for the changes in my life.

The lesson seems to be that there are times when you submit to God that He raises you up. I feel the closer I grow to God, the more that God is on view. I am not projecting myself but allowing myself to be transparent so that others can see God working. The more I refuse to stand up and speak under my own strength the more opportunities God is providing for me to be used. As I withdraw from the limelight, people seek me out in the shadows. It is humbling to watch how God uses what seem to be simple acts to touch the lives of others in the deepest ways.

God has a wonderful sense of humor. One of the men with whom I worked, a man who had been deeply into drugs and violence, has become a Christian. I took him through the twelve steps and Freedom in Christ.

The man has been sharing small bits in the workplace. He talked about a woman with whom he works who is on the verge of believing. She suffers from anxiety and has been seeking answers for peace in alternative religions. The man said he thought he would give her a Bible. I had a simple Bible which I said he could give to her if he would like.

I had picked up a coffee and pulled into a lay-by[20] and called the man to tell him I had the Bible. The man said he would come by to pick it up. He drove up in a big black car with tinted windows and we both rolled down our windows and passed the Bible from one car to the other. All of a sudden it hit us and we began to laugh. If the police came by, they would think the pages of that Bible were laced with

---

[20] A paved area at the side of a highway designated for drivers to stop in, for emergency parking, or where vehicles can wait,

some kind of drugs! Then the man asked, "How did this happen, Mick? How did we go from passing drugs to passing Bibles?" God changes people in a way that completely turns them around. Without being aware of it we were using experience from the evil in our past to impact others for Christ. We are both aware of the profound changes God has made in each of our lives and praised God together for those changes.

To love someone who is difficult, perhaps because of addiction, to really love him/her is to bring truth. I am involved with a man who is strongly addicted to gambling. He has lost his family, has no money. He has started going to church. Each week he spends all his money, cries, and then the church comes to his aid and allows him to not pay rent and they give him food. My personal experience as an addict has taught me that allowing dependence feeds the addiction, the person will literally swallow up whatever is offered, and he/she will never change.

One day I was with the gentleman and recognized instantly that all the man's money was gone. I asked, "You've spent all your money, haven't you?" The man replied he had and then added, "But I've only done it because I've been to the doctors and I got some real bad news; I've got diabetes." I put my bag down and sat next to him and said, "I've got something to tell you. I don't believe you. I think you are a very, very dishonest man and that you make stories up so that you can feel better about yourself. I think you are arrogant; especially around your gambler friends. You are very manipulative. You are manipulating the people who are trying to help you." The man looked at me and started to cry. As he cried, I asked, "Are these tears for people you have hurt, whom you have let down--your family, the people who are trying to help you? Or are these tears for yourself?" He said, "Why are you talking to me like this? Nobody's ever talked to me like this." I asked if what I was saying was true? The man replied, "Yes, but..." I said, "Let's just forget the 'but', is it true?" He looked at me and said yes. I then told him I wanted to ask him some questions and asked him to just answer yes or no. "Are you a thirty-two-year-old man that expects everybody else to pay your way in life?" He said, "Yes, but..." I said, "Let's forget the 'but'." The man said, "Yes." I said, "Did you plan yesterday before you got paid to go and spend the money?" He said, "Yes, bu..." I said, "Forget the 'but'." The man said, "Yes." I asked him if he thought other people should run around worrying about him, checking up on him, seeing if he had food, worrying if he was suicidal? Do you think this is okay? The man replied, "No, it isn't." The man asked, "Can you stop now?" I said, "No." I asked if he thought his mother cried at night because she didn't see him anymore? The man didn't answer. I asked if he thought his father was ashamed because he didn't have his son with him? I asked him what the real truth was? Instead of answering the question, the man replied he was feeling physically sick. I asked if he lived in a fantasy world which meant he didn't have to face the truth? The man didn't reply. I asked if he thought he pulled other people into this fantasy world—especially people who were trying to help him. He didn't answer. I asked the man if wanted me to stop asking questions? He said, "Yes." I asked him why? He said, "Because it's all true." I said, "Do you not know that the truth will set you free?" The man didn't understand. I said, "If you ask God what the truth is in your life; in your heart; things will change." I asked him if he would ask God to help him not hurt any more people. The man replied he would.

If one understands addiction as an illness resulting from sin, then you can speak truth into it. Sometimes we want to help people in our own strength by giving them things they don't need. We must allow God to show us what someone needs, not necessarily what they want, but what they need, and then speak and respond into that. If you see a homeless man with three cups of coffee, why would you buy him another cup of coffee? Telling the truth can be brutal but not if the truth is spoken in love and not in anger. I have met many people with addictive natures and found it very common for them to live in a fantasy world, that everything is going to be okay--by next year I'll be fine. It's a denial of the truth that becomes so entrenched that in the end the person cannot tell the difference between fantasy and reality. To humor someone who is suffering to that extent is wrong. The truth is not popular. Even in this situation, other people who had been trying to help this young man were not happy with me for making the man face the truth. However, the gospel of love demands truth. When we try to show the gospel in its fullness there are times that other people, sometimes even Christians, may be in conflict with us. I wonder: if you see someone suffering every day and could tell him/her a way to not be in pain why would you not tell them? What does the reluctance to tell the truth say about me? The man isn't ready to stop what he's doing; he just doesn't like the consequences. He needs to learn to take responsibility for his sin—arrogance and self-pity—in order to be able to be healed.

I received a phone call from someone I had helped from a place of using drugs and alcohol. This person had been an exceptionally violent man. I had the pleasure of sharing the gospel with him and his acceptance resulted in a complete change in the man's life. I was telling him that people were seeing things in him that they couldn't see before; that what they were seeing was God in his life—in his actions, his words, and in his eyes. I told him truthfully how he influences other people in a positive way because of his love for God. The man said he sometimes still gets angry and very frustrated, but for a different reason now. Now it's because he feels he knows the answer for people he loves who have big problems—he feels he knows the answer, but they won't listen.

As I reflected on the man's words, I recognized he has become a man of God and has become transformed by

God's love into a man who longs to serve. I wondered where I was—where we as Christians are—in the light of people who don't listen. I find I still have a rebellious spirit at times; a spirit that doesn't always want to submit to authority; a spirit that has a desire to rebel against social norms. Sometimes I want to do things my way. I know from Scripture and from my inner being that this is wrong and that it is sinful. I asked God to teach me how to lay myself down. I realized what I was experiencing was self-will and pride rather than the will of God. As I prayed, I was transported back in my mind to nine years ago and watched the journey from that time to where I stand today. Nine years ago, I saw myself with a gun in my hand, rebellious, no fear of God, no fear of anyone or anything—or so I thought—I just didn't understand what fear was. I began to realize that rebellion against God and the refusal to submit to authority was what took me to the point of planning to murder. I noticed how as God has been with me, the pride and rebellion have been more painful than they needed to be, because I still struggled to fully submit. This makes me identify more with the people who won't listen to God than with my friend who longs for them to know God and His peace. This friend helped me identify this sin and I have asked God to show me how to fully submit all things to Jesus. Even though my friend is a new Christian. he is teaching me and, because of my struggles over the years, I have learned to listen. The natural thing for me to have done was to go into teacher mode and agree that I know loads of people like this and here's what you should do, and here's the scripture, and put myself above him. But the ways of God are not like that. God is using this new Christian to teach me through the Holy Spirit. I need to listen, because if I can identify my own failings and give them to God, it makes my need equal to the people that turn away from God. In that equality of sin, I can be of real truthful service. Submission to authority and ridding myself of rebellion within is the best way to be prepared to serve. We need to become like the sinner because we really are the sinner and it's in that togetherness that we can give Christ to others in a truly powerful way that can transform people's lives.

Submitting to authority is not just following the rules. It is also recognizing that when we see people doing things they shouldn't do, we acknowledge, "So do I" and that makes us equal in our need to submit to Christ's authority. Submission to Christ's authority brings a deeper love and appreciation for the "sinners" around us which makes us approachable, and, therefore, makes the other person more open to hear the message of God's love.

It's this understanding and teaching in my life that has taken me from alcoholism, drug addiction, and excessive violence, to a place of peace, understanding, compassion, and empathy. These are all things I never possessed under my own strength—all are gifts from God—that have led me to restore relationships with family and friends. These gifts have allowed me to be able to have a loving and caring relationship with Sarah, not to rely on my own ability, but to trust God financially, physically, and emotionally, to learn to read, and to have no anxiety about life. These are such amazing gifts from God! Once I used violence to deal with the anxiety I experienced, and the absence of anxiety is in itself a huge miracle in my life!

One of the biggest things I have learned since becoming a Christian is being able to identify my own sin, acknowledge it, repent, and give it to God. The key is being grateful to God for showing me my own failings because that's what real love is—speaking the truth in love. When the Holy Spirit reveals our sin to us it provides the mechanism we need to come fully back to Christ. The humility we experience when we acknowledge and repent of our sin clears any separation between us and the Lord. If we rebel and don't accept the truth, we experience more pain and the gulf between us becomes greater.

This reminded me of another situation where the Lord used me to help a person become clean and sober and find God. As part of the process this man wanted to make amends to his mother for all he had put her through. His mother had experienced a severe stroke and couldn't talk properly. She had been ill for many years and suffered from a type of dementia which made her quite confused. We discussed how he could make amends to his mother. Would she be able to understand? Would it mean anything if she couldn't? Would it be pointless? We decided that it was up to God and the man should try to make amends. We thought that if his heart was right in the process, God would do the rest.

The man went to his mother and sat down with her and told he her had found God. He told her how sorry he was for all the things he had done that had hurt her. As he was feeling a genuine humility, he experienced a miraculous event. For the first time in many years he looked at his mom and her eyes completely changed—she spoke clearly, and they had a conversation like they hadn't been able to have for years. She was able to understand everything and talk with him. She told him she had always prayed for him and that she loved him. When they finished the conversation she immediately returned to her previous state. But he knew the amends had been made and received.

It seemed as through in his act of humility of actually making the effort to make amends, and meaning it, that God made the exchange between them possible. My friend identified his sin, repented, was truly grateful to God for showing him a better way, which resulted in a restored relationship. Within that process he witnessed a miracle that he uses to this day to testify to the power of God.

We cannot have humility in rebellion. We can only have humility when we lay ourselves down and submit. I praise God that I have found humility and have many chances to practice it. I also realize I can never live up to the true humility of God and feel I fail on many occasions. Faith alone drives me on and always quenches, fills, and restores.

PART THREE

Farewells, Reconciliations, and

Facing the Future

My dad, who was approaching ninety, had been in hospital. The medical system had mistakenly left in a tube that was supposed to be in for twenty-eight days for eighteen months. Dad tried and tried to get them to remove it and had even been hospitalized for recurring infections. He finally received a letter of apology and an appointment to remove the tube on an outpatient basis. However, medical personnel were unable to remove it as an outpatient surgery since it required the skills of a specialist. Dad refused to go home until it was removed. He ended up spending two weeks in the hospital and finally all of the tube was removed.

The day after the operation he felt really well. He had a very sound mind. He was sitting quietly beside his bed; praying and thinking about the suffering Jesus went through on the cross. He had come to faith within the last couple of years. His renewed relationship with me had resulted in him coming to know the Lord in a new and personal way. As he was praying, the nurse came over and said, "We were worried about you last night. After the operation your blood pressure was low. We got the doctor, and everything is normal now." Dad thanked her, and he remained in his chair thinking. He imagined Jesus sitting next to him. As he was doing that, he opened his eyes and it became real to him—he could see Jesus sitting there. As Dad was telling this to me, the tears were flooding down his face. I asked him what Jesus said or did. Dad replied, "Jesus said, 'I had low blood pressure when they scourged me, so I know what it feels like. When they nailed me to the cross my blood pressure went even lower, but I refused medication so that you could have it.' Jesus put his hand on Dad's shoulder and simply said, "You are one of mine." Then Jesus was no longer visible. Dad was transformed by this encounter and radiated God's love. He was very tired and weak but otherwise very, very bright.

I don't pretend to know what it means but know what I saw. I saw a transformed man who said, "And now I'm ready." Which I took as meaning he's ready to die. At this point he was still fit, not ill, not on a death bed, but he was prepared. He had received a second blessing. He appeared to be a sanctified person.

The love Dad showed following this occasion was different than it was before. He was now able to express love. Dad was brought up in a tough background where men didn't easily express their love—especially to their sons--perhaps to their daughters. But now he had no problems expressing his love openly to me. He's been overwhelmed with tears of joy. He has a new, deeper humility in his character. It's apparent that he made a total surrender to God which made him different from what he was before. I praise God that I have been able to see this change in my dad. I am especially grateful for the comfort Jesus gave to Dad through the slightest of touch on his shoulder and the simplest of words: "You are one of Mine."

I was thinking about the prodigal son. I had read the story, thought about what I had learned at NTC from a theological aspect, and then continued thinking about it more deeply. I thought about myself, coming as a prodigal son back to the church.

I was welcomed into the church. But I felt like there were a lot of "good sons" in the church. They were happy to have me attend but they would only accept me so far. I felt some exclusion from anything beyond community worship. When I showed any desire to naturally move to into ministry within the church, I was cut off. It hurt at first but then I became okay with it. Then I learned that someone else that I had helped on the road to recovery was experiencing the same thing. Welcomed, until he expressed interest in being involved in the ministry of the church, and then was shut out from being involved in any ministry other than what he was told to do.

It is almost as though fear moves in and stifles the Spirit. Some people feel threatened by someone who comes in from another background and is getting theological training. A fear that the "norm" will be challenged and require change. I wondered if they had ever been the prodigal son who became the good son? Each of us needs to ask: With whom do I identify? Was I once the prodigal son who has now become the good son? What part of the story do I play in the church? Am I the good son who feels a bit jealous? Or am I the father who welcomes with open arms, forgiving, and celebrating the prodigal's return?

As a church we need to examine ourselves and look at how we react to those who come home. At the same time, we as individuals need to extend grace to the church. Not turn away because our feelings get hurt but respond with mercy and humility as we work together to become the body Christ intended us to be. We are quick to welcome newcomers into the church but then what? Are we willing to acknowledge the spiritual gifts God has given them and allow them to use those gifts?

Some churches are making an effort to take the church outside the walls and that is a good thing. However, they often choose the leadership for that ministry from those long established within the church; "Jim" who has been an engineer for fifty years and loves the Lord but has no idea of what it means to live on the streets is chosen to direct the program, while "Chris" the recovered addict who has recently lived on the street is pushed aside—or allowed to come along to carry the sandwiches and coffee. "Chris" is not being mentored so that he can progress beyond that point, so he feels stifled. Eventually the "Chris's" leave the organized church and go back to minister to those on the streets on their own.

The unorganized street church is ministering to those on the street because they don't feel accepted within the organized church. God's work is still getting done, but by a different kind of church. There are many people who feel called to this type of ministry. They are out working on the streets, praying with people, meeting with other Christians to pray and work together, filled with the Spirit, working in obedience to God's direction, but they are not recognized as a church.

How do we unite the organized church and the street church--not necessarily to meet together, but to recognize each other as an important part of God's family? The problem for both the mainstream church and the invisible church is they are unwittingly creating a church just like themselves--exclusive. This is not right. We are meant to be inclusive, welcoming people from all backgrounds, all ages, all experiences, to learn more of God's ways and live and love as He commands us, so that as a united church we can take the gospel to every corner of the earth.

Where there is separation there is sin. For the invisible church the sin may be a rebellious spirit and failure to submit to authority. For the mainstream church it may be pride which prevents it from accepting the gifting from a different kind of community. God works anyway, but only by identifying sin can people repent, and it is only in repentance that healing and a coming together can be found. This takes us back to the story of the prodigal son. Which one am I? The prodigal son, the good son, or the father that brings everything together?

I was in a family situation involving serious illness. The person who was ill was having trouble accepting the reality of the situation. As I thought about the situation, I recognized the dishonesty of denial. I realized that I too had been in denial. Denial about how I really feel about how ill the person is; denial about how I feel about how that death may impact my life. Denial is very subtle. I don't know if it is a sin, but it seems a very subtle way of avoiding the truth. To try to live in "the day" one must accept what is real and what is true. I prayed that I could do that. The real truth was that it was overwhelming and consuming me. I felt like a huge weight was pushing on my chest. I felt fear and anxiety. I felt useless and the feeling got stronger and stronger. As I turned to prayer, I felt the weight getting heavier, not lighter. I felt like I was physically carrying a weight. I went to the college trying to carry on with my studies. I was very tired, trying to keep things afloat in my life. I sat down at the desk to write and couldn't even pick up the pen. I prayed. Then I got up out of the chair, walked around the library once, and as I was heading back to my chair, saw one of the librarians and asked her to pray for me right then. I told her the situation; told her how I felt; told her I thought I couldn't cope and that I wanted to run and not do the studies; not do anything; just ask the world to leave me alone. She smiled, put her hand on my shoulder and she prayed. I didn't even hear the words she said but the weight, the heaviness lifted with each breath. As I was breathing, I felt lighter and lighter. The lighter I got the more tears fell from my eyes. The tears went from tears of pain to tears of joy in less than a minute. There was no more burden to carry. My mind was completely clear. I instinctively knew what I had to do. I got extensions for my essays; put things in place to make myself more available if necessary; and accepted life as it really was. Once again, I had been transformed. The heaviness did not return, and I knew exactly what I had to do.

I am slowly realizing that the cross of Jesus Christ is most certainly personal, but you can only experience it fully in community. It was another Christian that spoke the words I couldn't on my behalf. It was that coming together equally that seemed to speak to God and the prayer was answered instantly. More and more I am coming to believe that "I" am not the church but most certainly "we" are. I still battle against being involved in conventional church but in truth know that is where I am being drawn. I thank God for a community of believers.

I really believe that we must be vulnerable; we must be truthful. Denial of the truth is blinding. When you come out of denial and realize that you have no power on your own you can then rely on God's power. Then things can change.

I realize that just locking myself up in prayer and praying for hours at a time has value, but it isn't living out the gospel to its fullest. It's participating in life that reveals Christ. You spend time alone with God in prayer so you can become vulnerable enough to love your neighbour when in community.

When I came into some unexpected money, I bought my finance a gold cross. She in return gave me one that she had. I've had interesting experiences with crosses. I've never bought one for myself. It's either a cross that someone has given me or one I've given to another person. Sometimes I have taken it off my own neck and placed it around the neck of another. There seems to have been power in that act; not for me but for the other person.

I was at a church cafe where I meet up about once a week with a couple of people to pray. As I went in to pray an elder of the church and a young man teetering on the edge of faith were there. The young man asked the person how he should pray. The elder had written down the Bible reference to the Lord's prayer and the Bible reference to prayer in Philippians and as they sat down at the table the elder asked me, "How do you think he should pray?"

I asked the young man if he wanted to pray because he was afraid, or did he want to pray because he loved God. He replied that he was afraid. I asked him what he was afraid of? The young man replied that he got paid the next day and he was afraid he would gamble all his money away. I had the cross that Sarah had given me around my neck. I took it off and put it on the young man. I pulled him toward me and kissed him on the top of his head. I told him that he was now a brother and when he felt the urge to gamble just to hold the cross and ask Jesus to help him. The young man cried and cried. He said, "So that's how you pray then?" I asked, "What do you mean?" He said, "You love somebody like Jesus loves us." I said, "That's exactly it." It was evident that the Holy Spirit was in the place. However, it was also obvious that the elder of the church was not happy with what had happened. As I thought about what happened, I was reminded of a text I had received a few days previously. I showed the young man the text which read, "Thank you Mick Fleming. God bless. I am traveling up to Wales today and some days I feel I owe it all to an amazing guy who loaned me a crucifix and gave me hope. Much love, Michael. God bless you always." I had sent the man a happy birthday text and the man reminded me that five years before he had been a heavy heroin addict that couldn't stop using, couldn't get clean. I had a cross around my neck and took it off and put it around the other man's neck. I told him when he was one year clean that he was to give me back the cross. The man said he thought he would be keeping it forever. I said, "No. You'll definitely be giving it back." When he was one year clean, he met me and put the cross back around my neck and fastened it for me. As I shared this story with the young man in the church café the young man told me he felt different, that he was feeling warm inside. I know the power is not in the piece of metal; I know that I am not the power; but I also know that we are called to share everything that we are and everything that we have in a way that honours God. The young man touched the tattoo of the cross I have on my hand and said, "He's always with you, isn't He, Mick?" I felt this feeling of real humility and real love. I felt I was learning so much from this young man. He was teaching me truly how to pray. When he looked around the room and thought about things and bowed his head in prayer, I knew that the young man who had come in and asked us how we should pray was the one doing the teaching. I thanked God that I could see that.

I am learning that even in the church there is a resistance to change; a feeling of being threatened by someone from the outside who expresses their faith in a different way. The tendency is to feel hurt and shut out when this happens, but in reality, it may be a call from God to be a loving change-maker within the body. A call to become involved in a way that forgets self and loves others as God directs us to love. In accepting those who agree with us while praying with and for those who see things in a different light allows the Holy Spirit to reveal truth.

As I was coming to the end of my studies, I began asking myself more and more, "What is church? What does it mean?"

My initial experience of church nine years ago was a feeling of separation—I didn't feel a part of what was going on. Although the churches I went to were always welcoming, I felt I was some sort of project to the other Christian people—let's help the poor addict. I know now that wasn't really true but that it was my own blurred vision—I was the one who was prejudiced. I was still seeking self-sufficiency and not God sufficiency. I wasn't like those people and, therefore, they couldn't possibly understand me. Although I felt I was a Christian I sought solace with other suffering, struggling people like myself because I could feel broken with them, and I really was. We could pray equally with each other. I did not feel that equality in the church. My church became the streets, the homes and opportunities to be with people who were struggling in everyday life. I had an attitude of wanting to create a church with people just like me. I realize now that is not a church.

I started to understand diversity of faith, to learn other people's belief systems. One day during prayer I recognized a deep rebellion against the middle classes within church which had led to my resistance almost to a point where I felt "They won't change me; they won't make me middle class", because that's what I felt the church was trying to do to me. The wonderful thing about the Holy Spirit is that He uses even one's sin for good. He convicted me of my resentment toward the middle class through people whom I considered to be middle class Christians. These middle-class Christians genuinely loved me and didn't want to change me. I realized one day, through the kindness and love I had been shown, that the gospel has no class system to it—there is no hierarchy in the Kingdom of God. I realized from that point on that I can't be a Christian alone—I need the community so the Spirit can convict me of my own sin. How can I love my neighbour if I'm the one choosing who my neighbour is? The example of my middle-class Christian friends--who really weren't middle class, they were just Christians—was the real catalyst that opened up to me what church should look like.

As I have lived in Christian community at NTC and my studies are coming to an end, I've been drawn more and more to attending regular church. I'm smiling as I say this, as

I've been asking myself why I send so many people to churches and get them hooked up, but yet wasn't regularly going myself? What a hypocrite! It's been the unveiling of what the people of God actually are that transformed me again and took me closer to God and to the will of God.

While I was praying about my connection with church I was questioning where I belonged and asking why I didn't fit in? What were people in churches doing and were they doing it properly? I saw a distinct misconception of addiction within addiction ministries. I wanted to be part of this institution but refused to surrender myself to it. As a result of earnest prayer, I am pleased to say I have now surrendered myself to church. I now recognize the value of the church. I clearly see that all the way through my rebellion against the church, people from the church provided me with gospels, financial support for my ministry to people in the streets and those with addictions, and they have bombarded the Lord with prayer on my behalf. All along the church was working for me—I just didn't recognize it as the church because, to my failing, I saw individuals and not the body of Christ. I am still repenting and surrendering this over to God and accepting the grace God is pouring into me. Sarah and I have now been welcomed into a wonderful church. It is a church that seems to want to encourage and build us up. A church which asks us to participate and to give of ourselves to others. This blind Christian finally feels as though he has come home.

Principles and not personalities are a big concept. I know I have been flawed in my thinking as I now realize how much I need others. The church is where one can be taught about the gospel and the early years of the church and learn how that impacts our walk today. I am drawn to the command in the third chapter of Galatians to never forget the poor. I now realize the poor are not just the materially poor but those who are poor in the spirit of life. James and Peter shook hands and made a contract with Paul that he was to take the gospel to the Gentiles but admonished him to not forget the poor.

I have finally recognized my former prejudice against the church, and I have been able to leave it behind and recognize the truth of the church and my need to be part of a Christian community. I couldn't see the love I received because of my blindness caused from seeing the one person that did it wrong. Although there have been times when I might have been held back from ministering within the church, my own prejudice against those I felt were judging me actually made it worse. As the Lord has opened my eyes, I now see the part I played and recognize my need to be part of a Christian community and to work together to better represent Christ to others.

I realized how controlling I have been in my life. I feel I have been obedient to God; and as much as I am able to understand, I am obedient to God in my actions. But it's not always the actions that are bad or sinful, but rather the spirit in which things are done.

I find that people who irritate me or don't fit my mold of thinking are the ones that have been my greatest teachers. I used to pray for forgiveness for my feelings toward these people and then I realized that the Lord had provided me with the best teachers I could ever imagine. My prayers began to change; I began to thank God for clearly showing me my own sin. I stopped trying to be nice to these people—because it was fake—and decided to be truthful in what I believed God was saying to me.

Because I was thanking God for putting these people in my life to show me my own sin, I began to thank the people who were irritating me. I became very honest with them, not about their defects, but with my own. I saw this not only changed me but also transformed others. The people I resented became people I love. It's the topsy-turvy world of God. There are days when I forget but then I go straight back to God, straight back to the drawing board, and surrender it all over again.

God has granted me the grace to love the bossiest, most obnoxious, and controlling people –to hold them in my arms and for us to cry together. We are now able to surrender our pride to each other, each acknowledging our own sin and forgiving the other for his/her sins. When I do meet people like this, I thank God for showing me something within myself that needs to change. I become honest with myself that I don't have patience, that I'm becoming resentful—and God shows me what is wrong within myself. Not what's wrong with the other person, but what's wrong with me.

The first two levels of honesty are the easiest two—even though they are difficult. The third level of honesty—one that we don't always get to, is being honest with the person you resent. That honesty is not about them but about you. To be able to become vulnerable with that person confess that sometimes you get angry or frustrated with life and ask them to pray for you. The third level of honesty acknowledges your own sin. When one accepts these three levels of honesty and acts upon all three, the transformation is remarkable. There is room in the relationship for God and when God is in it nothing else can get in the way.

It's important to remember it has nothing to do with the other person's faults. When we are being honest it is important to be honest in a humble and gentle spirit. We are telling the truth about our own sins, we are not talking at all about the other person's faults or sins, we are confessing our own. When we ask the other person to pray for us it creates a bond and through that bond the Lord knocks down the wall between the two and we are free to love each other in a fresh and honest way. We no longer must pretend to be nice. We can love each other with a love that comes only from the Lord. When we are just trying to be nice it is really hard work. But when we allow the Lord to work in any relationship, we don't have to pretend to be nice, God will show us how to genuinely love. I have said to people, "Sometimes I just get wound up and get angry. Would you pray for me?" Often the response will be something like, "I know what you mean, I can be a bit like that myself." And when we pray for each other it is a mutual prayer for each other instead of a self-centered prayer of being about me. It's important to stop pretending that we love people when we really find them difficult and irritating and want nothing to do with them. We must ask God to show us how to be real and loving in our relationships.

As I come to the end of my schooling, I'm not sure what is ahead. How do I listen to God? Am I missing what He's saying to me? How do I know it's God and not just my imagination? How do I know that I am living in God's will and not self-will? God speaks to us when we lay ourselves down physically, emotionally, mentally; when we put ourselves to one side. That is not allowing yourself to be walked over but serving lovingly and also having the courage and wisdom to speak against injustice; knowing what is right and what is wrong.

When Paul talks about his gospel of powerlessness, how he is Christ crucified, it was because he had put himself to one side, became powerless, and, as a result of the suffering he encountered, was joyful. He was full of joy in spite of the suffering.

My experience has been that with Christ I don't really feel I am suffering as I just feel more loved when I am suffering.

Jesus pours more love into me. Therefore, the more I suffer the closer to God I am. If that is true with me than it is also true with everyone else. Therefore, I seek out the suffering people because my desire is to be as close to God as possible and it is in this process and interaction that God speaks to me so crisp and clearly, so beautifully and gently. My experience is that when it relates to service for God, He always speaks. When it relates to service for myself, it is my mind, my wants, and my needs that are speaking and not God. Therefore, it is loving in suffering that leads to a deeper love of God.

Sarah and I were talking, and she said, "You are so lucky! God seems to speak to you so clearly." I replied, "The more I pray, the more I read the Bible, and the more obedient to God I try to be, the luckier I get." She smiled.

There have been times when God has spoken to me as clear as crystal through the Scripture. It's almost been, "Look at that!" Undeniably speaking to me through the Word. But most often He speaks to me through other people. The questions that I address to God are usually answered through interaction with other Christians; sometimes ridiculously randomly.

One day another student was in the library and when I sat down the student said, "God spoke to me about you, Mick." I said, "Go ahead." The student said, "When God speaks to you Mick, it is truth." I agreed. The student continued, "So don't pretend it's not true." I said, "What do you mean? Can you give me an example?" The student said, "God said you should be ordained. And you should kick doors down so that it can happen. He's told you that it's going to happen so you should kick anything out of the way that would keep that from happening." We both realized that the Holy Spirit had spoken through the other student and we hugged and wept.

The following Sunday I was at church and they asked if anyone wanted to come forward and pray. I got up without planning to and went to the front. As I prayed, I spoke fearlessly from Galatians 2. Nothing like this had ever happened to me before. It was like I was wondering, "What on earth am I doing?" When I finished, the congregation stood up and clapped, which is something I certainly did not expect. The worship had been wonderful and though the gospel was being preached, something seemed to be missing. I was reminded of Galatians 2 when Paul went to the apostles and James told him not to forget the poor. I felt compelled to say that any gospel that forgets the poor is not the gospel; I felt compelled to say it. It is about Jesus dying and His resurrection, but it is also don't forget the poor. And God will show us who the poor are--it is not necessarily just materially poor. If we forget the poor, no matter how much we sing and dance and praise, we are not really worshipping.

I had been at this church for a month. Sarah and I didn't know anyone when we went through the door, the people in the church didn't know about our pasts or my studies. Within four weeks the pastor was talking about me being ordained and I was standing up preaching! I had never preached in a church before.

Later that same student revealed to me that the Lord had also spoken to him and said he needed to acknowledge that God had given him the gift of prophecy, but he was afraid to speak it. When he spoke to me, he knew that God wanted his obedience in this area. I shared with the man that he was the second person in two weeks to speak to me about ordination. It was something I was beginning to accept.

When God speaks, it is for something that is going to benefit others and not something for a selfish use. God wants servants; people that He loves-- and that love must be mutual. He wants the best for all.

God has given me everything I need—and more. But none of it is for me. Everything is a tool to serve—whether to my son, my family, or for people outside—everything is given for that purpose. I am blessed only so I can bless other people and that's how I know it is from God. Whether that be money, time, advice—it will always be mutual, and it will always to be to bless others.

Sometimes when God speaks to us, fear stops us from listening. If you can find out what you are afraid of and ask God to take that away, His voice will become clearer. Fear can be unrecognized. It is the complete opposite of faith. The fear to stand up front and preach is not there now—but it used to be. The fear that God might change my life in ways I am uncomfortable with is gone. I find that when I recognize fear in my own life and give it to God, God takes the fear away and my faith gets deeper and stronger. I am then able to see and hear God working in my life. Crucially, I am also able to respond in obedience.

There are times when I physically want to give or do something for God and it's not what God wants. In those instances, I also must listen to God to hear what God wants, because God is teaching me. What is my true motive in serving? If my actions are not motivated by love, peace, joy, gentleness—I need to rethink what I'm going to do. I stop and turn to God. On many occasions I have given like a fool, not like a servant. When I give like a fool that is not God, that's me.

Many times, God teaches through our mistakes. We have to go to Him first to get the right answer. There are times when obedience is instant and there are times when it is not, for when I don't know whether it's me or God, I have to go and ask God for clarity.

Early one morning I was sitting in McDonalds having a coffee. I looked and across the restaurant saw a man and a woman dressed in heavy coats and hats in the blazing sunshine. That was unusual and out of character. As I looked closely, I could see that they were heavy drug users. I knew I had to do something, knew that God wanted a response from me, but I didn't know what it was. I asked God. I opened my Bible and there was the scripture, "Feed my sheep." I smiled to myself. The guy got up to go to the toilet and as he approached my table, I stood up, made full eye contact with him, and said, "How are you doing?" The man replied, "I am very hungry." I told him I would like to buy breakfast for them. I bought them breakfast and was amazed because I have no money and shouldn't even be able to feed myself, and yet God had provided, and I obeyed. I thank God for that. They sat down and ate their food, still across the restaurant. The man I had spoken with looked at me and tapped his hand in the spot where I have a cross tattooed on my hand. I just looked at him and put my fist to my heart and tapped it. I felt I had given the full gospel.

God had spoken, I asked what I should do, God told me, the people got fed, and they recognized it was through Christ. I heard God speak and I felt His love. Because they were blessed, so was I. The full gospel message includes, "Don't forget the poor."

I was sitting in a church service where they were reporting on a recent mission trip to Hungary. They had shared about the manifestation of the Spirit, how people had come to the Lord, been baptized, and how these people, who were really materially poor people, had looked after and fed them. They felt honoured by the people they had gone to serve.

The Holy Spirit had definitely given the gifts of encouragement and prophecy to one of the elders who was speaking. As I was listening to him share about the trip, I got a picture in my mind, which had never happened to me before, of the speaker with stones in his hand and he was planting them in a field. The thought came to my mind that the man had two gifts and it was now the physical gift God wanted him to use. I had a vision of the man's hands—that God wanted him to use his hands.

When the elder finished speaking he came and sat down next to me and said, "At the end, don't leave, I need to talk with you." At the end of the service the man told me that he felt God had spoken to him. He felt God wanted me to know that I was going to be given two opportunities in church leadership, and God loves me so much that He wants me to have a choice. Both choices are of God and He is giving me the opportunity to choose. He asked me if that meant anything and I shared that since I was finishing my studies and have no idea where I'm going it was really encouraging. The timing of what he said was perfect. Then I told him what I had seen in my mind. The man thanked me and became emotional and I realized it had meant something to him.

On Sunday evenings I am usually tied up with a one-to-one ministry. However, that evening my appointment was cancelled and I decided to attend the Sunday evening service for the first time. When I arrived, I found it was a set up for what I thought was a café church but there were microphones on the table. It turned out that it was set up for a global radio program.

The elder that I had spoken with in the morning was sharing that when he was in Hungary he was in the field and he looked across this field and "thought I was going bonkers" because he saw three holy men, shepherds, but they were not flesh and blood, walking around the boundary of the field. He felt that this was the spot where a physical church was going to be built. As he was speaking, he looked at me and said, "I am a bricklayer; now do you understand?" I felt teary and emotional as I realized that God had spoken through me. I felt humbly peaceful deep inside myself.

Someone texted into the radio show and said, "If God's working like that overseas why is He not working like that in your own locality?" Another of the church elders who was sitting next to me put his hand on my shoulder and said, "I think Mick's going to tell you about that." It was a surprise to me as I hadn't planned to speak at all! But I was able to share some of the events recorded in this book and said, "God's working like that everywhere. You only have to open your eyes, be obedient, and not be afraid, and you will see it."

The bricklayer said he thought God was calling the people who had recently started coming to this church to unite them in a common purpose. This included he and his wife, Sarah and I, and some others who seemed to have been directed to this church. This was no mistake or fluke. He pointed to me and said "We've all noticed how Mick prays and what happens when he prays. Let's not pretend we haven't noticed, because we have." I didn't understand what he meant but knew I was being encouraged.

I find in worship it is much easier for me to listen to God than to speak to Him. And the word of God always moves me to tears and emotion. This is the same whether I am worshiping in private or with others. I recently heard that true prayer involves listening even more than speaking. It's more important to ask God what or how He wants us to respond than why things are happening. It brought to mind one of my favorite sayings: Take the cotton out of your ears and put it in your mouth!

After the service the man told me that he felt the words I had given him were definitely from God. He is nearing retirement age and has enough money to meet his needs. He feels that God is telling him he is to go and physically use the skill of his hands to build the church. Now God just needs to convince his wife!

I was in another church service and during a time of prayer was motioned to come up and join others who were praying for a man. I went forward to join them in prayer. The man had been involved in an accident some years ago and had suffered pain in his back and shoulder. The people were praying directly for the pain to be removed when I was asked to join them. I then experienced something that is relatively new to me and only happens when I am asked to pray for someone. As I put my hands on the man's shoulders and was about to pray, instead of praying for the healing of his back and shoulder I was directed to give the man intimate details about his past relationship and asked God that the man would be able to forgive for what happened in that relationship. I told the man to breathe in and breathe out. I said, "As you start to breathe in and out you will start to feel the Lord healing your body. I want you to breathe in heavenly love and breathe out forgiveness." I asked him if he could feel anything changing in his body and he nodded his head. He affirmed that he was feeling intense heat in his shoulder and his back and all he could say, over and over again, was "Thank you, Jesus! Thank you, Jesus!" Afterward the man put his arms around me and held me so tight. He no longer had any pain. For me this is something that is very special, but it is something I have no power or control over; I can't go to people and tell them anything. I don't get to choose the people or what to say. It is humbling to know that God can do these things; I can't manufacture or do anything on my own. It's only when God tells me to speak and gives me the words. It's like God is taking authority over the situation and uses me—but it is not my authority, not my decision to take authority—it's the authority of Jesus at work. It's not until I reflect afterward that I realize that God has taken over and used me. It's a new experience but I know it is God, not me.

Human faith comes to an end. There is faith beyond human faith, and I am beginning to feel a taste of that—of stepping into heavenly faith and that's where the power is. We barely touch it. It is when we use our own faith as much as we can but then give the situation to God that we get recharged with a greater faith.

Another time when I was at church a family from Hungary was preparing to move back and asked for prayer. The pastor was preparing to pray with a woman using an interpreter when he motioned for me to come up and join him. The pastor told me to put my hands on her shoulder while he prayed. He prayed, and the interpreter prayed with him. When the pastor had finished, I had a vision of a young girl sitting in the field surrounded by beautiful flowers, happy and smiling. The Lord stood above her. I asked the interpreter to share it with her and the woman for whom we had been praying burst out in tears. I took her into my arms and the interpreter told me the woman's sister had recently died, and my vision had given her hope and comfort. It seemed to deepen her faith in Christ. I can feel my own faith deepening. It's the kind of faith that **knows** that Christ is real and through Him all things are possible.

I was asked to give my testimony on the radio. I said I would if I could bring Sarah so that her testimony could be heard as well. I feel her innocence of faith and the love she has to share with others is a voice that needs to be heard, especially by women. I was able to touch on some things that have been shared in this book. Sarah was able to share how we met, the circumstances, and the miraculous work that the Lord has done in both of us—separately and together. After the show we were asked if the two of us would be interested in having our own radio show. The man asked us to pray about it, saying what we are doing on the street is great, but we could reach so many people through radio. I had once thought it would be very cool to be on the radio. The Lord is giving me the things I once wanted for my own purpose in new ways, to bring glory to Jesus. I will wait for the Lord to reveal if we are to serve this way.

I must give myself to the Lord every day. It's still a battle to remind myself that nothing I do or have comes from me, but from Jesus. My desire is to give God all the glory, but I can only do that when I recognize the truth in myself and rebuke anything that would take glory from God.

Pride seems to be the worst sin. Unless we are honest with ourselves, we cannot spot it within ourselves. The denial of what's in me is often accompanied by "I'm not that bad" but it's recognizing, admitting, and asking God to remove the pride that focuses on ourselves. Accepting the sinfulness of pride and asking forgiveness brings peace and restores a right relationship with Jesus. It's something we all need every day.

At Dad's ninetieth birthday party all the family were gathered together to celebrate. There was an atmosphere of genuine warmth. When I was hugging my grown children, I could feel there were no longer any barriers; nothing in the way. I noticed when I looked at the photos there were no forced smiles. They were genuine smiles and filled with love.

Halfway through the celebration Dad suddenly passed out. My sister and I took him, knelt, held him and prayed. He started to come to. The paramedics had been called and said he needed to go to the hospital as his blood pressure had dropped very low. But Dad asked if he could have some pie first and they said of course. The paramedics sat down and patiently waited, as part of the party, while he had his pie. The two weeks previous Dad had lost his voice, he spoke very croakily, one had to listen carefully to understand what he was saying. Before Dad left the party, he asked me to thank everyone for him and I did. I spoke a few minutes about what it means to be family, what it meant to belong to a family, I was looking at Dad, reflecting, and I really didn't know what I was saying. As I spoke people were crying but I didn't know why. When Dad left in the wheelchair, he did it in triumph, raising his arms like a champion as he left!

The morning after, which happened to be Pentecost Sunday, Sarah and I were sitting in church when Dad phoned and in a very low-pitched, hard to hear voice, said, "Come and see me now." We left church and went to the hospital. Dad told us he had terminal lung cancer which had moved

174

into his throat, he could die at any moment and he was full of joy as he spoke. He was ecstatic with the love of God! He said, "I can't wait to start my new life with Jesus!" He laughed and told me, "I'm going to see Him before you do!" Then he asked me to bring my youngest son Jack right away so he could speak to him.

I went and picked up Jack, whose mother also has cancer. On the journey back to the hospital I explained the situation to him, and he was devasted by the news. Over the past three years Dad, Jack and I have gone out once a week and have become very close as we shared life together, discussing football, and all the things going on in our lives.

When we arrived at the hospital Dad asked Jack to sit next to him on the bed and said to him, "I want to tell you something that it's taken me a lifetime to learn. I want you to really listen to me as it is really important. You have got to learn to love. You have got to pray every day that the Holy Spirit will show you how to love everyone you meet that day." Jack enjoys boxing. Dad said to Jack, "When you are boxing someone, you are punching them and actually trying to hurt them. But what happens, Jack, when the fight's over?" Jack said, "You hug him, you put your arms around him." Dad said, "Do you do it whether you win or whether you lose?" Jack said, "Yes." Dad said, "Then live like it's the end of the fight, not the beginning." Jack understood what his granddad was saying. Jack started to cry, and granddad and grandson sat hugging each other. Dad said, "Don't cry for me. Don't cry for yourself—cry for the people that don't know Jesus because they are the ones that are worthy of your tears. Do you understand Jack, that you can't love like this unless you know Jesus?" Jack said he did.

When Jack and I left the hospital, I sensed a difference in Jack, an acceptance that wasn't there before. It seemed like his fear for his granddad had been lifted. Jack commented that there was a big difference between his granddad and some others he knows who are facing death. I asked if he knew what caused that difference and he said, "Yes, Dad, I do." I didn't need to say anything, Jack understood that Jesus makes the difference.

The love that Dad had discussed with Jack has impacted him so much that he too wants to share it. Jesus is very infectious. And I have been reminded that it is because of the love I shared with Dad that he was able to discover the love of Jesus.

That evening I went back to church for the evening service. After the service one of elders came and asked if I would pray for him and his wife. I said of course but felt quite humbled that they had asked me to pray for them. They sat down, and I asked what they would like me to pray for. The man said years and years ago he and his wife had been prophesied over that they would be involved in a ministry of healing and deliverance and it had never happened. He felt with it being Pentecost that if we prayed, they might be released into that ministry. I began to pray with the two of them and as I prayed, I saw a black oblong gob inside the man, and I asked if the man would put his hand on his chest in that spot. As I prayed out loud, I said, "Lord, I can see something, and I don't know what it is. Lord, tell me what it is." Immediately the answer came to my mind and the words came out, "You had a terribly, terribly abusive father." Then I put my hands on the man's shoulder and started to pray. As I prayed the man wept bitterly. I held him in my arms, cradling him in the love of Jesus. As I continued to pray, I took hold of the man's wife's hand and put it on top of the man's hand and the words came again. "Can you forgive your husband for his harsh treatment of your children?" The couple put their arms around each other and wept. I also wept as I put my arms around the two of them. I prayed for peace and love. Within the prayer I explained to them that when Jesus forgives us for what we have done, also the sin that has been done against us loses power. I then prayed that God would completely remove the power of sin. When we finished praying the man shared that he had had a horrendously abusive father; he said, "You couldn't have known these things, Mick, so it must be God." They had asked me to pray for their ministry in deliverance and healing, but the man felt that he had been the one who had just been delivered and healed.

On Dad's actual birthday all his children visited him in the hospital and celebrated with balloons and a time of reminiscing. Although we knew he had cancer the doctor had now confirmed that it was in his liver, his stomach, his lungs, and his throat. When we asked the prognosis, the doctor said Dad could live for as long as three months, but he couldn't be sure; it could be sooner. Dad looked so disappointed. I held his hand and asked him what was troubling him. He replied, "I want to see Jesus sooner than that. I was hoping it would be like a few days. But His will, not mine. I think the Lord still wants me to learn perseverance." And then he smiled again.

The family gathered around the hospital bed in the private room to pray and I suggested we hold hands. Before we prayed Dad said, "Mick, open the door so people can hear." We opened the door and then joined hands as I began to pray out loud. I could feel the Holy Spirit and experienced the change of atmosphere with the white noise that I have experienced at other times. When I hear that noise, I don't know what I'm going to say or do but I have learned to recognize that the Holy Spirit is actively involved in what's happening. As I prayed, and I don't remember the words I prayed, I knew the Holy Spirit was in the room, everyone else in the room was weeping. As I finished praying the room was filled with emotion and I turned to my youngest sister who was standing next to me. She had been teetering on the edge of faith for a long time. I put my hands on her shoulders and looked her in the eyes and said to her, "Are you sorry for everything you have ever done wrong in your life?" She said she was. "Do you believe in Jesus and that He is the Son of God?" She said yes. I told her that Jesus forgives all your sins and He wants you to feel the same love that Dad feels right now. She broke down in tears and accepted the Lord completely. For the past few days she had been blaming God, asking Him, "Why are you doing this to my dad?" She said she was beginning to understand. She said she felt all fizzy inside. She'd been set free. Her bitterness is gone, and she is significantly different and testifies to feeling different. I gave her the Gospel of John and she is reading it and asking questions.

As Dad's life was coming to an end, I was seeing Romans 8:28 played out: God is working, and for those who love God all things work for eternal good. I see the power of Christ's love flowing through my family, transforming our lives, and spreading that love to others with whom we come in contact.

A few days later Dad's nurses were saying it could be weeks before he died—they didn't know. But the next Saturday when I went to visit, Dad said, "I'll be gone for dinner, I'll be having dinner with your mother." We prayed together. I had a Gospel of John in my pocket and I read to Dad about how Jesus died.

The family gathered to be with him, all my children, and my sisters. Dad held on until he saw his last daughter arrive and when she came in, he took her hand and within two minutes he had breathed his last. It was so peaceful. I had whispered in his ear how Jesus was waiting to welcome him home, I described how mom would look, how she would smell, and Dad started to smile. I said, "Look, who's running toward you, so excited to see you, the daughter that died in your arms is running toward you with her arms wide open, look, you've fallen into her arms now."

Dad had an audio book player that was unplugged, turned off, with no batteries. When he died, it turned on for about 30 seconds and then turned off. It seemed the life energy as Dad passed brought a burst of energy to the innate object. It was noticeable how easily and well he died; he didn't even gasp for air. He took his last breath and didn't breathe back out.

The fact that Dad waited for his last daughter seems to have had a special significance to the family. We feel it was a divine appointment, that he'd been waiting for her. This daughter has begun to ask questions about faith. I have no doubt that the Lord will reach her with His love; I can see her softening, asking questions.

It seems a certainty that all my family will come to the Lord—something I never thought possible—for myself, Dad, or my sisters. As Dad passed away mom's prayers were answered in full and the family was once again reunited in faith and love. Her prayers passed beyond the grave and that helps me to understand that love never dies. Love has eternal life. The ultimate expression of love can only be found in the life, death, and resurrection of Jesus Christ. I know this is true because I have tasted and found it was good.

After Dad passed, the family sat down to talk about the funeral, possessions, etc. and we were all united. It was the first time we had all been able to sit down together without someone getting angry and storming off. It was the first time we had all been able to pray together. My sister who recently accepted Jesus had been reading John and was so happy with her new faith, singing praises to Jesus. I gave this sister Mother's Bible. I felt it was right for her to have it.

The theme of Dad's funeral was love and joy and it was a celebration of a changed life. I was able to read from 1 Corinthians 13 what the Bible has to say about love. In addition, I knew I was to say a few words at the end of the service. I had been praying about it but had no idea of what I was going to say. As I stepped up to the microphone, I was asking God to give me the words. The words came and I shared how Dad had asked how my life had been so changed; what really happened? I said it was Jesus. Then Dad asked, but what really happened, what made so great a change? He had witnessed an amazing transformation in my life and wanted desperately to understand what made the difference. I had told Dad to close his eyes and put his hand on his heart and feel it beat. I said, "That's life that you are feeling there. Try to understand that you don't have any control over it; you can't stop your heart beating." Dad nodded in agreement. Then I asked him to think about all the people that he loves or had loved in his life, whether living or dead, and to notice his heart was still beating and to notice how he felt different as he was thinking about the people he loves. I then told him to think about the people he'd hurt, think about the things he had done that he was not proud of. I asked him if the love he felt was big enough to say sorry to those people. He nodded in agreement. I could see emotion building up in him. I then asked him to think about all the people who had hurt him, think about all the things that have been done and said against him. I could feel the atmosphere changing and sensed the presence of the Holy Spirit. I asked if the love was big enough to forgive those people. He nodded his head in agreement and began to weep. I said, "Dad, what's the name of this love?" He replied, "Jesus." I held him in my arms, and we wept together. Afterwards I asked him how he felt, and Dad replied, "Forgiven! Why did I not know about this? All of my life--why did I not know about this?" And I assured him, "But Dad, you do now." I closed with, "If you know the name of this love then you are truly blessed and if you don't, may you find Him now." As I sat down, even the officiating priest seemed moved and just sat there for a few minutes before bringing the service to an end.

As I stepped down from the pulpit I felt as though I had stepped into new skin. Everything that had happened was not who I had been, not what I am comfortable doing. But suddenly everything felt "right"—the suit, speaking God's truth in simple terms, reading the Word with conviction—it seemed as though God was showing me this is what I am meant to do. At this point I don't know what that means, can't really express what I was feeling, but through things that have happened in the past few months I believe God is calling me to a new work—not yet revealed, but slowly coming to life one step at a time.

Following the funeral, I learned that some people had left as they felt convicted and others felt liberated and free. Many began asking me questions. They felt something during my prayer, and they wanted to know what it meant. Many people have contacted me and asked to meet with me—the people I thought most unlikely to ask these questions and say these things. There is power in the gospel whenever it is shared, wherever it is shared. We must never be afraid to share the power of the gospel and what real love is. Until we understand the fullness of God's love and what it really means we do not understand the gospel—we are just reading from a book.

One Friday after Dad's death I was walking through town on a busy afternoon wearing a suit because I had an appointment. There was a lady begging. She was very ill--yellow, jaundiced, all the physical signs of being close to physical death--a very, very ill lady. I sat down next to her and began talking with her. I asked her what she needed, asked her if she had ever been in love, asked if she felt anyone in her life had truly loved her. She said she wanted to cry because of what I had said but she couldn't. I told her I understood. As we were talking, a very well-dressed, attractive, very smart-looking lady walked past. Then she stopped and turned around and walked back. She bent down, looked me right in the eyes and said, "You are a good man." Then she stood up and walked away. A tear ran down my face because she saw only a man in a suit sitting on the floor but the lady I was with was invisible to her. It made me think how we take attention from the needy. The tear was not because she said I was good man but because she didn't see the woman sitting beside me, dying, needing attention—she only saw the suit.

The following Saturday morning I felt lost. This was the day I usually spent with Dad, taking him shopping, just spending time with him. And now, especially on the weekends, I pray for opportunities to be with people, to be filled with God.

The night before I had been reading in James how true faith compels you to love. So, I went out and saw a different homeless lady. This time I was wearing combat pants and a tee shirt; I blended in very nicely with the surroundings. I sat down beside her, asked if she would like a coffee and some food. She said she would like some coffee. I got us each a cup and as I sat down, I asked her to tell me about her life. As we were talking, two other homeless people came up and sat down with us. I included them in the conversation. I like to talk with people who are struggling with things they never talk about, such as what love is. They usually talk about where they can get a drink or score, but people don't talk to them about important things. I asked them if they thought there was a better life for them, or did they think that was only for people who were rich or had jobs. Then three more homeless people came up and joined us. We were starting to fill in a circle. They also joined in the conversation. They were telling about some of the good times they had experienced in their lives.

Finally, I asked them, "Sometimes when you go to sleep at night, and maybe you are cold, or need a drink, or maybe took some drugs, do you ever pray?" I asked because when I was homeless, I sometimes used to pray. I didn't know to whom I was praying or what I believed in, but sometimes I would pray. Every one of the people sitting there said they did pray. I told them I thought God was really, really, close to them; that God was with them. One laughed and said, "Why do you think that?" I replied, "Because where there is anybody suffering you will find Jesus." The man dropped his head and started to nod in agreement and just at that point a man walking by dropped some change into the hat that was on the ground.

As he was walking off, I said, "Excuse me, but do you believe in God? We are just having a conversation." The man replied he didn't; he didn't think there was a God. One of the homeless men said to him, "There is a God and his name is Jesus and He is with us when we don't have anything." The man sat down and asked him what he meant. I sat back and listened as all the homeless, addicted people told the man what they thought about Jesus and God.

The gathering sitting on the ground outside McDonalds began to draw attention. People were coming over to put money in the hat, but really, they were using that as an excuse to find out what was going on. Another lady joined the conversation and said she believed in God. She squatted down, not sitting but still she entered the conversation. Then another man walked past and dropped some money in the hat, and I asked him if he believed in God. The man replied he most certainly did. I said to him, "Since you believe in God would you pray for us all?" So, on the street outside McDonalds a man stood over the group and prayed for us; the homeless, the broken, the working, the non-working, the black, the white, the hungry, the full—he prayed for us all— we were all the same. Then the man pulled a small Bible out of his pocket and shared a few verses of scripture.

A small gathering had just happened because I sat down. We were all equal. Nobody saw a suit; the focus was God. In that time, fifteen to thirty minutes, nobody was homeless, nobody was hungry, nobody was arrogant—there was only love. As we started to disperse, people started shaking hands and hugging each other as they left. Homeless and those with homes alike.

The lady that I had originally sat down with began to sob and asked what had just happened. I replied, "Perhaps you've just realized that Jesus really does love you and you are as good as anybody else. Jesus is with you." I gave her a gospel of John and told her, "If you ever get time, read it, and when you read it, remember this feeling you have now, and you will read it differently." And then I left. As I was walking away, she shouted, "What's your name?" I replied, "Mick". She said, "Mick, come here." I turned back. She said, "Look what's happened," and she pointed to the hat—it was full. None of them had noticed but as they were talking, people were walking by putting in money and there was a lot of money in the hat. She said, "Mick, Jesus has filled my hat!" I replied, "Love Him and it will never be empty."

As I walked away, I realized how I would fill the time I used to spend with Dad—I would now spend the time with people who needed their hats filled up--no suit required.

The truly remarkable things I have seen in my life, where people have been freed—the most wonderful things are the simplest. To share a coffee with a stranger, to smile as you are walking down the street at someone you don't even know, to stop and help someone with a flat tire, to see someone struggling and ask if they need any help. The most wonderful gift that God gives us is the ability to listen and when we truly listen to other people, we can hear God speaking. Understanding love as being far bigger than myself and my own needs has awakened my spirit. I have learned to thank God for the simple, everyday things in life. This has allowed me to see more of God.

As I prepare to complete my degree, have buried my father, and am about to move to a different city, I am unsure of the next step. I was praying to take the right step and to walk in the will of God. The minute I finished praying I received a text message which read, "His Lord said to him, 'Well done, good and faithful servant. You were faithful over a few things; I will make you ruler over many things. Enter into the joy of your Lord.' Matthew 25:21" Although that scripture didn't say do a, b, c, d, it gave me confirmation that what I have been doing is right and I am going in the right direction. The person who sent me the text has never rung or texted me before. He is someone from the college who took my number six or eight months ago and we haven't spoken since. I called him and asked him what moved him to send the text. Did he send it to everyone or was it a personal one for me? He said, "Mick, I don't know where you are in your life, but I felt God told me to send you this."

So, I still don't know the answer, but I know God is with me. That is as simple and as assuring as it comes.

EPILOGUE

On October 6, 2018, I was awarded the Degree of Bachelor of Arts (Honours) in Theology from Nazarene Theological College, Partner of the University of Manchester, Manchester, England, United Kingdom. I became an ordained pastor in March 2019. I have since started Church on the Street in two towns in Northern England with help from volunteers from various denominations. I planted Burnley Community Church which meets in the Gannow Community Centre as well as an evening Recovery Church which meets in a Methodist centre. There is **still** power in the name of Jesus!

Printed in Great Britain
by Amazon

68681291R00108